Leo
2000

By the same author

TERI KING'S COMPLETE GUIDE TO YOUR STARS

TERI KING'S ASTROLOGICAL HOROSCOPES FOR 2000:

Aries 21 March to 20 April
Taurus 21 April to 21 May
Gemini 22 May to 21 June
Cancer 22 June to 23 July
Virgo 24 August to 23 September
Libra 24 September to 23 October
Scorpio 24 October to 22 November
Sagittarius 23 November to 21 December
Capricorn 22 December to 20 January
Aquarius 21 January to 19 February
Pisces 20 February to 20 March

Teri King's Astrological Horoscopes for 2000

Leo

Teri King's complete horoscope
for all those whose birthdays fall between
24 July and 23 August

Teri King

ELEMENT

Shaftesbury, Dorset ● Boston, Massachusetts
Melbourne, Victoria

© Element Books Limited 1999
Text © Teri King 1999

First published in Great Britain in 1999 by
Element Books Limited
Shaftesbury, Dorset SP7 8BP

Published in the USA in 1999 by
Element Books, Inc.
160 North Washington Street
Boston, MA 02114

Published in Australia in 1999 by
Element Books and distributed by
Penguin Australia Limited
487 Maroondah Highway
Ringwood, Victoria 3134

Teri King has asserted her right under the
Copyright, Designs and Patents Act, 1988
to be identified as the author of this work.

All rights reserved.
No part of this book may be reproduced or utilized
in any form or by any means, electronic or mechanical,
without prior permission in writing from the Publisher.

Cover design and imaging by Slatter-Anderson
Design by Mark Slader
Typeset by Palimpsest Book Production Limited,
Polmont, Stirlingshire
Printed and bound in Great Britain by
Caledonian International Book Manufacturing Ltd, Glasgow

British Library Cataloguing in Publication
data available

Library of Congress Cataloging in Publication
data available

ISBN 1-86204-437-6

Element Books regrets that it cannot enter into any correspondence
with readers requesting information about their horoscopes.

Contents

vii
Introduction

1
How Does Astrology Work?

5
The Sun in Leo

7
A Fresh Look at Your Sun Sign

16
The Year Ahead: Overview

20
Career Year

23
Money Year

28
Love and Sex Year

34
Health and Diet Year

38
Numerology Year

61
Your Sun Sign Partner

73
Monthly and Daily Guides

Leo

24 July – 23 August

Ruling Planet: **The Sun**

Element: **Fire**

Quality: **Masculine, Positive**

Planetary Principle: **Creativity**

Primal Desire: **Power**

Colours: **Red, Orange, Gold, Yellow**

Jewels: **Amber, Ruby, Chrysolite**

Day: **Sunday**

Magical Number: **19**

Famous Leo
Jacqueline Onassis, Princess Margaret, Mae West, Benito Mussolini, Alfred Hitchcock, George Bernard Shaw, Napoleon Boneparte, Henry Ford, Percy Bysshe Shelley, Robert Redford, Andy Warhol, Dustin Hoffman

Introduction

ASTROLOGY HAS MANY USES, not least of these its ability to help us to understand both ourselves and other people. Unfortunately there are many misconceptions and confusions associated with it, such as that old chestnut – how can a zodiac forecast be accurate for all the millions of people born under one particular sign?

The answer to this is that all horoscopes published in newspapers, books and magazines are, of necessity, of a general nature. Unless an astrologer can work from the date, time and place of your birth, the reading given will only be true for the typical member of your sign.

For instance, let's take a person born on 9 August. This person is principally a subject of Leo, simply because the Sun occupied that section of the heavens known as Leo during 24 July to 23 August. However, when delving into astrology at its most serious, there are other influences which need to be taken into consideration – for example, the Moon. This planet enters a fresh sign every 48 hours. On the birth date in question it may have been in, say, Virgo. And if this were the case it would make our particular subject Leo (Sun representing willpower) and Virgo (Moon representing instincts) or if you will a Leo/Virgo. Then again the rising sign or 'ascendant' must also be taken into consideration. This also changes constantly as the Earth revolves: approximately every two hours a new section of the heavens comes into view – a new sign passes over the horizon. The rising sign is of the utmost importance, determining the image projected by the subject to the outside world – in effect, the personality.

The time of birth is essential when compiling a birth chart. Let us suppose that in this particular instance Leo was rising at the time of birth. Now, because two of the three main influences are Leo, our sample case would be fairly typical of his or her sign, possessing all the faults and attributes associated with it. However, if the Moon and ascendant had been in Virgo then, whilst our subject would certainly display some of the Leo attributes or faults, it is more than likely that for the most part he or she would feel and behave more like a Virgoan.

As if life weren't complicated enough, this procedure must be carried through to take into account all the remaining planets. The position and signs of Mercury, Venus, Mars, Jupiter, Saturn, Uranus, Neptune and Pluto must all be discovered, plus the aspect formed from one planet to another. The calculation and interpretation of these movements by an astrologer will then produce an individual birth chart.

Because the heavens are constantly changing, people with identical charts are a very rare occurrence. Although it is not inconceivable that it could happen, this would mean that the two subjects were born not only on the same date and at the same time, but also in the same place. Should such an incident occur, then the deciding factors as to how these individuals would differ in their approach to life, love, career, financial prospects and so on would be due to environmental and parental influence.

Returning to our hypothetical Leo: our example with the Sun in Leo and Moon in Virgo, may find it useful not only to read up on his or her Sun sign (Leo) but also to read the section dealing with Virgo (the Moon). Nevertheless, this does not invalidate Sun sign astrology. This is because of the great power the Sun possesses, and on any chart this planet plays an important role.

Belief in astrology does not necessarily mean believing in totally determined lives – that we are predestined and have no control over our fate. What it does clearly show is that our lives run in cycles, for both good and bad and, with the aid of astrology, we can make the most of, or minimize, certain patterns and tendencies. How this is done is entirely up to the individual. For example, if you are in possession of the knowledge that you are about to experience a lucky few days or weeks, then you can make the most of them by pushing ahead with plans. You can also be better prepared for illness, misfortune, romantic upset and every adversity.

Astrology should be used as it was originally intended – as a guide, especially to character. In this direction it is invaluable and it can help us in all aspects of friendship, work and romance. It makes it easier for us to see ourselves as we really are and, what's more, as others see us. We can recognize both our own weaknesses and strengths and those of others. It can give us both outer confidence and inner peace.

In the following pages you will find: personality profiles; an in-depth look at the year ahead from all possible angles including numerology; your Sun sign partner;

monthly and daily guides; plus, and it is a big plus, information for those poor and confused creatures so often ignored who are born on 'the cusp' – at the beginning or the end of each sign.

Used wisely, astrology can help you through life. It is not intended to encourage complacency, since, in the final analysis, what you do with your life is up to you. This book will aid you in adopting the correct attitude to the year ahead and thus maximize your chances of success. Positive thinking is encouraged because this helps us to attract positive situations. Allow astrology to walk hand in hand with you and you will be increasing your chances of success and happiness.

How Does Astrology Work?

YOU OFTEN HEAR PEOPLE say that there is no scientific explanation for astrology. However, astrological calculations may be explained in a very precise way and they can be done by anyone with a little practice and a knowledge of the movement of the stars and planets. It is the interpretations and conclusions drawn from these observations that are not necessarily consistent or verifiable, and, to be sure, predicted events do not always happen. Yet astrology has lasted in our culture for over 3,000 years, so there must be something in it!

So how can we explain astrology? Well, each individual birth sign has its own set of deep-seated characteristics and an understanding of these can give you fresh insights into why you behave as you do. Reading an astrological interpretation, even if it is just to find out how, say, a new relationship might develop, will make you think about yourself in a very deep way. But it is important to remember that the stars don't determine your fate; it is up to you to use them to the best advantage in any situation.

Although astrology, like many other 'alternative' subjects, such as homeopathy, dowsing and telepathy, cannot completely be explained, there have been convincing experiments that have shown that it works far more often than chance would allow. The best-known studies are those of the French statistician, Michel Gauquelin, whose results were checked by a professor at the University of London who declared, grudgingly, that 'there was something in it'.

An important aspect of astrology is to look at how the Sun and the Moon affect the natural world around us, day-in-day-out. For instance, the rise and fall of the tides is purely a result of the movement and position of the Moon relative to the Earth. If this massive magnetic pull can move the oceans of the Earth, what does it do to us? After all, we are, on average, over 60 per cent water!

When it comes to the ways in which the Sun influences the world, a whole book could be written on the subject. The influences we know about include daylength, heat, light and solar storms, as well as magnetic, ultra-violet and many other forms of radiation. And all this from over 90 million miles away! For example, observation of birds has shown that before migration – which is governed by the changing of the length of days – they put on extra layers of fat, and also that they experience a nocturnal restlessness shortly before setting off on their travels. I'm not suggesting that we put on weight and experience sleepless nights because of the time of year, but many people will tell you that different seasons affect them in different ways. Another example is a curious species of giant worm which lives in underground caverns in the South Pacific. Twice a year, as the Sun is rising and the tide is at its highest, these worms come to the surface of the ocean. The inhabitants of the islands consider them a great delicacy! There are so many instances where the creatures of this planet

How Does Astrology Work? 3

respond to the influences of the Moon and the Sun that it is only common sense to wonder whether the positions of other planets also have an effect, even if it is more subtle and less easy to identify.

Finally, we come to the question as to how astrology might work in predicting future events. As we have seen, the planetary bodies are likely to affect us in all sorts of ways, both physically and mentally. Most often, subtle changes of positions of the planets will influence our emotional states and, of course, this will affect how we behave. By drawing up a chart based on precise birth times, and by using their intuition, some astrologers can make precise observations about how planetary influences in the years ahead are likely to shape the life of an individual. Many people are very surprised at how well an astrologer seems to 'understand' them after reading a commentary on their birth chart!

Stranger still are the astrologers who appear to be able to predict future events, many years before they happen. The most famous example of all is the 16th-century French astrologer, Nostradamus, who is well-known for having predicted the possibility of world destruction at the end of this millennium. Don't worry, I think I can cheerfully put everyone's mind at rest by assuring you that the world will go on for a good many years yet.

Although Nostradamus certainly made some very accurate predictions in his lifetime, his prophecies for our future are very obscure and are hotly disputed by all the experts. Mind you, it is quite clear that there are likely to be massive changes ahead. It is a possibility, for instance, that information may come to light about past civilizations, now sunk beneath the Mediterranean Sea and this will give us a good idea about how people once lived in the past, and provide pointers as to how we should live in the future. Try not to fear, dear reader. Astrology is a tool for us to use; if we use it wisely, no doubt we will survive with greater wisdom and with a greater respect for our world and for each other.

The Sun in Leo

It's likely that you need a trolley to carry all your charge cards. You feel you always have to look your best, which could be dangerous because you would knock down two little old ladies in a supermarket to avoid your current heart-throb if you felt that you were looking anything but your best.

You usually see the world as a brilliant widescreen movie. Because of your detached awareness of yourself, you have a fine sense of humour and usually laugh the hardest when your larger-than-life drama turns into a three-ring circus. You imbue life with a lustre that others find so appealing that they often form a fan club. You never have to go looking for excitement because you can find it anywhere, even at the laundrette or in a queue at the check-out. Your constant *joie de vivre* and enthusiasm dazzle the crowds of people moving through your life, and because of this it seems to some that you are impervious to pain. Actually your pride and need for privacy are so great that you don't easily show more deeply felt emotions.

The opposite sex most often confuse the strength of your personality with the strength of your passion, and often mistake impersonal warmth for seduction tactics. However, what you enjoy most is the dramatic game and the persuasive tactics that other people use to ensure your presence. You adore love if it shimmers with glamour and reeks of the romance of a midnight movie, otherwise you are indifferent to cheap dinners and 10 o'clock phone calls enquiring if you'd like company.

You're independent and ambitious. Your prime goal is leadership on a grand scale. Your difficulty, however, is that you can't appreciate your successes on a small scale. As you drive yourself up the ladder of success, try not to lose your mental flexibility, otherwise when you finally get to the top you may find that you are king or queen of an empty kingdom.

A Fresh Look at Your Sun Sign

As a rule, members of the general public appreciate and understand that for practical reasons Sun sign astrology is fairly general, and therefore for a more in-depth study it is necessary to hire an astrologer who will then proceed to study the date, year, place and time of birth of an individual. Then, by correlating the birth chart with the positions of the different planets, a picture can be drawn up for the client.

However, there is also a middle way, which can be illuminating. Each sign comprises 30 'degrees' (or days) and, by reducing these down into three sections, it becomes possible to draw up a picture of each sign which is far more intimate than the usual methods. Therefore, check out your date of birth and draw your own conclusions from the information below.

Leo (24 July to 23 August)

Born between 24 July and 4 August
Your Sun is in the first section of Leo. This suggests that your ego needs are very much stronger than those of the

Leos born later in the month. Intense pride galvanizes you towards the goals with which you hope to gain the recognition you so desperately need. Sometimes you are almost possessed, driven on by egotistical dreams. You could be likened to a machine that is out of control and unable to stop until it has run its course.

Because you genuinely believe that leisure time is a waste of time, unless it means the opportunity to meet the 'right people', you rarely consider holidays unless they are somehow connected with your job. This is the nearest you can come to being lazy without breaking out in a nervous rash caused by boredom. It is likely that all your life those closest to you have begged you to relax. However, being a tense extrovert, you have worked your way to maturity in spasms of vitality that usually end in complete exhaustion.

You are optimistic, enthusiastic and interested in literally everything around you. You probably have sufficient activities planned to keep you busy well into your nineties. This is because you can't find a way to fit them in any earlier. You are idealistic, positive and highly aggressive. You possess the knowledge to transform ideas into reality and your mind paves your way with the right attitude. You are generally able to get what you want out of life because you never consider the possibility of failure; the only factor that you dwell upon is time. While there are occasions when you want to stop the world, you will refuse to get off.

Born between 5 August and 15 august

You are born under the second section of Leo and so are friendly and happy-go-lucky with an irresistible sense of humour. You enjoy making other people laugh and you are good at it. This is because you are able to see the positive side of any situation. You radiate a brightness and you manage to maintain this, even when confronted with the gloomiest of situations.

You try hard to find a greater meaning to your life than you could ever expect to find on a material level. Metaphysics, religion, philosophy and the occult are some of the areas in which you may become engrossed in order to find some important answers. The more you mature, the more you realize the importance and significance of a further education. At this point, study in many forms begins to hold greater appeal, and the stimulation it causes can help to provide financial support during those times when everything seems to be against you.

Quite obviously then, you possess a strong inspirational streak which other people both envy and admire. You have a steady sense of purpose, and this, when combined with your faith, invariably seems to help you through. Because of all this, it is very common for you to find yourself in the position of confidante, helpfully listening to other people's problems and attempting to offer practical advice where possible. The more flappable and nervous types sense your inner strength and this draws them strongly to you. Quite often they just naturally assume that you can find the answers to life's problems and that your own life is running on well-oiled wheels, which isn't always the case. Deep within the inner reaches of your being you have a healthy lust for life which rarely deserts you, no matter what your age. However, unlike the Leo born during the first section of this sign, you also experience a deep sense of pleasure from the simple things in life. While you share an abundance of nervous energy with the first section, you seek to balance the time dedicated to work with other interests.

Tennis, yoga and Tai Chi are activities that hold a strong attraction for you and which could help you to release some of those inner tensions. Travel too plays an important part in your life and each trip is treated not simply as an opportunity for enjoyment or relaxation, but also as a learning experience.

Born between 16 August and 23 August

Your Sun occupies the third section of Leo. You are a dynamo running at full tilt and woe betide those poor idiots who try to get in your way. This section has overtones of both Leo and Aries, for you have the most determined aggression which is directed and motivated by the most powerful of wills. There is an inclination for you to live on a treadmill of continual activity which you relish. Although your friends and colleagues are likely to fall by the wayside or faint with exhaustion at the very idea of the jobs you so easily take on. This both confuses and irritates you, because you know that the harder you work, the greater your vitality and energy. Unlike the first section of Leo, who works simply for the sake of ego, you do so for the pleasure of the activity.

It has to be said that you are not easy to spend time with, because your high energy leaves other people miles behind you. They may try to keep up but generally fail to do so.

Because of all this, you can be quick-tempered and abrupt, and you dislike people who laze around yawning.

Since your mind moves at the speed of sound, those poor creatures who talk slowly and repeat their point over and over again simply make you twitch with irritation.

You do your best to avoid lazy individuals, clocks and telephones. Your idea of sheer hell is being waylaid by whiny, lazy people who repeat every sentence at least five times. The only thing you will listen to is illness, not because of the illness itself, but because it makes you slow down.

You are a demon for changes and challenges. Situations that would cause other people to retire hurt get your body and mind dancing. You deal with each emergency, tragedy and upheaval with the greatest of ease. What really gets you depressed is a period when nothing seems to be happening. But with your bravery, faith, will, drive and tenacity you will never be depressed for long. You are adaptability personified, resting only to regenerate yourself for the next cycle of challenges which you know are heading in your direction.

When you are bad you are very very bad (<u>Horror</u>scopes)

When you blow your top, you are inclined to dismiss people from your life. Then, some time later, while they are busily packing their luggage, you tentatively tap them on the shoulder and ask them where they think they might be going.

Your pride is so intense that it can make you climb mountains and with your determination and vitality you will very likely arrive at the top before any helicopter could. However, your lack of patience with less motivated people around you will send you stomping away, twitching and fuming. The least you expect is that your contacts be psychic because, after all, answering questions is extremely time-consuming. The people in your circle are expected to move at your pace.

Should you be more of a lazy lion, you plop your body down on to a velvet sofa while you fantasize about the energy being consumed at the health club. That is about as near as you are going to come to actually joining.

You can be bombastic, prone to exaggeration and unbelievably bossy. You instinctively feel that you are made for the better things in life, which you spend a lot of time creating. Your partner, colleagues and the family cat treat you unquestionably as master and stir up a constant stream of air by rushing around and tending to your every whim. Your employees mutter that you are a slave-driver, for while they are frantically trying to attend to one of your demands, you in the meantime are bellowing because they are not attending to their job. However, after a while they become acquainted with the idea that your basic motto in life is 'the world is my servant'.

Unfortunately, you can be insatiably disloyal and unfaithful. You tell yourself that you need intense action in every area of your life, and for someone who is as romantically alive as you are, marriage will rarely be able to offer enough.

The types you are drawn to are the more flashy, expensively dressed ones. It is of the utmost importance that whoever you spend your time with looks good, because it is important to you what other people think. Watch out, though, as all the rich food and booze can soon age your streamlined body.

Luckily, being conveniently short-sighted, you excel at overlooking your bulging thighs or stomach, which slowly hamper your ability to walk. Rather you will prefer to spend your time explaining to one of your many admirers how they are sadly losing their shape. Tact was never one of your virtues and the tender feelings of another human being are rarely taken into account. You believe that if someone can't take the truth then they should just remain stupid and suffer the consequences. It is strange how you can be so enamoured of the 'truth' yet at the same time lead a life so full of deceit. Luckily, most reasonably intelligent human beings are aware of the fact that your fiery temper is only another form of your need to be in control, but that by its very existence it suggests that you are totally out of control yourself. Underneath that angry glance is a frustrated infant who wishes he or she knew what to do next.

The kindest comment that can be made is that your insensibility is obvious to all around you. This is more than irritating, its embarrassing because it suggests a person others should feel sorry for, but never fear.

Your egotistical rages are little more than a display to prove to yourself that you really are in control. However, it is only a matter of time before those around you are exhausted by your repetitious performances. Eventually your emotional immaturity will betray you and the people who remain in your life will be the ones you need but never really desire. However, you fool yourself by quickly inventing lies to obliterate the lonely feelings you are experiencing. Nevertheless, your way of proceeding through life does get you from day to day and has you firmly convinced that eventually you really are going places.

Cusp Cases

Leo/Cancer Cusp: 21–26 July

If you are born under this particular cusp then it is quite obvious that you wear your heart on your sleeve like a designer label. The emotion and intuitiveness of the Moon-ruled Cancerian mixed here with a Leo solar light can give dazzling results. Your Cancerian intuition naturally tunes in to the needs of those around you, while your Leo magnetism attracts a large following. You care passionately and intensely about everything in which you are involved, and therefore complete all of your projects efficiently and with a certain style.

You enjoy power and have a great innate ability to lead. It is true that some of you may appear on the surface to be shy and retiring, but underneath it is likely that you are simply waiting for the opportunity to shine.

The place you call home is sure to be sensational, with Cancer's nesting instincts combined with Leo's dramatic flair for décor.

Leo/Virgo Cusp: 21–26 August

The Virgo shrewdness controls the extravagant Leo ways, and this can result in a successful business combination. Out of working hours, you settle for only the best, but modify those regal tastes by buying at the best price. You look for an impressive mate who will help you climb the social ladder, but take care not to be too demanding of your partner. You love to communicate and you are likely to be a good writer. It would be a good idea to keep a diary while you are living it up as this could lead to profit in later years. With your strong and erotic sense of fantasy, your partner will wait by the mailbox for your steamy love letters.

The Year Ahead: Overview

It is generally thought that no one can stand before you without instinctively straightening their shoulders and drawing themselves up to their full height. Your faith and trust in humanity, your serene conviction that those who are working for you will do their best, and that even those who fail you will do better in the future, all combine to waken a generous response in the heart of others. You give courage to those around you and set them striving to fulfil your expectations.

Multi-faceted yourself, you understand and appreciate the qualities of all kinds of people, and never waste time by asking from anyone what is not in their power to give. Therefore you are particularly successful in organizing activities and distributing duties. Commands, to be effective, must be easily understood and so your style is simple and straightforward. Approval is definite and unmistakable, and displeasure is conveyed without hesitation.

This year should be a good one, because there is a distinct possibility that you will gain from your own personality and the way you express yourself. You seem to be in control of your own fate, so when things go well you can pat yourself on the back but also take

The Year Ahead: Overview

responsibility when they don't. Where you may lose out this year is through any kind of partnership, legal affairs or committed relationships. If you're single, there may be several broken relationships because you're not going to be easily satisfied. In the main, it would be better for you to walk the path of destiny on your own. You may also run across opposition from time to time, and where work matters are concerned it would not be a good idea to form partnerships because they could be costly disasters.

This year the planet of change and upheaval, namely Pluto, will be coasting along in the fiery sign of Sagittarius. Activities in this part of your chart include all kinds of creativity, enjoyment and pleasure, love and romance, and also children. These areas will give you one or two heart-stopping moments but if you're prepared to put in the energy that is needed, then you should have nothing to fear.

Neptune, the planet of deception, illusion and escapism, also falls in the part of your chart devoted to partnerships. It's quite obvious that in this area you will not be thinking as clearly as you usually do. Your emotions will be riding on a roller-coaster but at least you're not going to be bored.

Uranus, the planet of sudden interruptions and surprises, will be squatting in the house of partnership too. It is obvious that there's going to be a great deal of emphasis on this side of your life during the year 2000 and there may be sudden attractions and repulsions. If you're already in a relationship, it could go through extremely rocky phases from time to time, but if it is based on understanding and true love then it will survive. Should you be single, however, you'll be drawn to others who may not necessarily be the right types for you, but enjoyable and interesting nonetheless.

That task master of the zodiac, Saturn, will be situated at the zenith point of your chart, and so of one thing you can be quite sure, this is not a year for being lazy or looking for the quick way out. Hard work is expected and if you accept this without complaint then eventually it could lead to promotion, even if that means added responsibility; but you like a challenge and this shouldn't faze you at all.

Moving on to Jupiter you may find this enormous planet in a changeable mood. In January through to 15 February it can be located in the fire sign of Aries. Certainly a good omen if you're doing any kind of travelling, dealing with foreign affairs or involved in intense studies. Your efforts will pay off at this time so keep at it. From 16 February till 30 July it will have moved into the zenith part of your chart. Now, if this isn't a good omen for promotion and general good luck, then I don't know what is. If you are out of work at this time, it's a period for pushing ahead for all your worth because you're sure to find yourself in the right place at the right time eventually.

From 1 July through to the end of the year it's the Leo who works in research, administration or as part of a team who will be positively shining. Should the latter apply, then there's no point in trying to lord it over other people as you sometimes do. Listen to what they've got to say, they're speaking a great deal of common sense and their words can certainly help you. Avoid any temptation to make a bid for power or dominance otherwise you may find yourself out in the cold and you will only have yourself to blame.

The Year Ahead: Overview

The year 2000 holds a great deal of promise, certainly there will be pitfalls from time to time, but you're optimistic and strong enough to take these in your stride and not allow them to depress you. After all, when it comes to life, if you run into a troubled and difficult period just wait a little while, because you can be quite sure that things will change. This year they will likely change in your favour if you are not lazy and are prepared to get out into the big wide world and really get stuck in. Neither should you be discouraged when other people seem to be attempting to pull you down. Believe you me, this is only jealousy at work and it should be completely ignored. Don't waste your time in petty squabbles, you're bigger than that. For a more in-depth look, please turn to the *Monthly* and *Daily Guides*.

Career Year

YOU'RE THE SORT OF CHARACTER WHO really needs to be out front, preferably with people who have to defer to you. This is because you want to rule the world and not just a cosy corner. Fame and glamour have beckoned since you were about four, but it is difficult for you to make decisions about your destiny because there are so many different avenues you would like to go down. Wherever your objectives lead you, the gates to fame will open with a resounding crash when you arrive.

Both directing and acting are definite considerations, since you've always loved the limelight. Professions which allow you to deal with the public are also a possibility. You tend to be rather people oriented and with your sense of luxury you could be very effective at influencing the consumer. Your sense of colour and beauty will serve you well in positions ranging from writing holiday brochures to fashion designing, from selling orchids in December to interior decorating. Then there's always painting, preparing new kinds of perfume, literary works of genius and, of course, teaching, because you excel at telling people what to do.

If you don't run the company, the chances are you'll own it. You're always a boss one way or another and love to give orders as much as you love working. People who are idle or lazy irritate you to distraction.

During the year 2000, Uranus and Neptune are in your opposite sign, so you may be drawn to a partnership in some form or another. Naturally, of course, you will expect to be the senior partner, but if I were you I'd keep this secret to yourself. At least give a show of cooperation as well as listening to others' ideas, because after all they could be equally as valid as your own. However, even if they're not, you may be able to take their little gems, develop them and turn them into something really special.

Should you work with children, animals or in a job associated with entertainment, then there may be some dramatic changes taking place from to time. However, though something may come to an abrupt end, do try to keep optimistic because this will be quickly followed by a new beginning. You will find yourself faced with a fresh challenge, which is something that you thoroughly enjoy. Sports people will be doing well, too, with the exception of certain periods which you can discover in the *Monthly* and *Daily Guides*.

Those of you who are hoping to get some kind of promotion may be lucky during the first few months of year. After this, though, you may need to content yourself with working for future recognition rather than for immediate advancement. Whatever you do for a living you may perhaps become involved more than you would like with administration. It's all very well painting on a very large canvas, but all of us have to deal with the nuts and bolts of life even if we don't like it, whether that includes hanging around for other people to make up their minds or dealing with administrators. You must try not to ignore this unpleasant side of life, so deal with it. This will help to smooth your progress a great deal, let me assure you of that.

Those of you who can convince yourself to stick to a reasonable timetable without being tied to it should do well. Even so, there may be a certain amount of upheaval from time to time, especially in your relationships with your workmates. However, there's no reason why the year 2000 shouldn't be an exceptional one, and, remember the stars may impel but they certainly don't compel.

Money Year

WHEN IT COMES TO MONEY YOU have to be honest and admit that you're not able to hang on to it for very long. Even when you write a cheque you do it so quickly the amount is immediately forgotten and the same can be said for your credit card. Certainly, you prefer convenience buying which very often means not remembering how much you've spent until you receive your bank statement. Well, at least there's one thing to be said for your sign, you're certainly not one of those people who will ever whinge that you don't know where you money has gone. With you it's certainly not a mystery, it's usually in your wardrobe or in your home. Money is merely a means to an end to you, and shouldn't be left sitting by itself in the bank.

Your money planet is, of course, Mercury and in January it will be situated in Capricorn up until the 18th. There's a suggestion here then that you may gain from people you are financially dependent upon. But there's also a possibility of a loss through officialdom or a bureaucrat. If I were you, I'd get out those tax forms and if they seem to be Arabic then give them to somebody who can explain them, so shelve that Leo pride.

In February Mercury will enter the water sign of

Pisces on the the 5th. This seems to suggest that you'll be getting an above average number of letters, and perhaps demands, from official sources. Whatever you do, don't make paper aeroplanes of them and throw them into the rubbish basket, otherwise there'll be trouble. Mind you, there is one bright spot, that is that people you are financially dependent upon, whether it's your partner or boss, seem to be doing extremely well. Also, they are ready to give you advice if only you can bring yourself to ask.

During March, unfortunately your financial planet, Mercury, will be in retrograde action until the 13th. Therefore, avoid major purchases or spending lavishly on entertainment, including romance. Once this planet sees sense on the 14th things assume a better perspective and, although you'll never be a saver to beat all savers, at least you are prepared to pay your bills; with any luck you'll have a little bit left over for some fun, especially if you happen to be socializing with people connected with your job.

April is a time when your thoughts will be turning to your summer holidays. However, if you should book during this time then you will, of course, be looking for the best rather than a bargain. The question you need to ask yourself though is: can you really afford it? If not, try to lower your sights a little, it is after all the company that you are keeping and the place that you are visiting which are the most important things. If you can't afford a luxury room on an enormous liner, it's not the end of the world. As long as you get to those sunny climes and enjoy yourself that really is all that counts, and you don't have to break the bank in order to do that.

In May there are no less than five planets coasting along through the zenith of your chart. This seems to suggest that you're working as hard as you possibly can, perhaps because you have a special purchase in mind. When a Lion really puts its mind to any kind of job, you can bet that it'll be done with the greatest efficiency, flair and will engender a great deal of admiration. However, don't become so money oriented that you neglect other sides of your life or you might not be too popular.

Financially, you need to take care during June. Certainly it's fairly routine up until the 23rd, but once Mercury goes into retrograde action bills that you had hoped would never arrive begin to pile up and you may even waste money on shoddy goods. You must not sign any kind of important financial document at this time, because you will live to regret it for some time to come, so do your best to take this advice.

Mercury resumes direct movement on 17 July and so after this date you are free of paperwork worries and may also travel. If you go before this date, you'll be storing up a great deal of aggravation for yourself. There's a strong possibility here, too, that other people will be only too willing to waste your money for you. Venus will be in your sign for the first two weeks and so it will be an easy matter for people to persuade you to spend. If ever there was a time for saying 'no' this is most certainly it, but if you don't, well then I can't answer for the consequences.

August, of course, is your time of the year and with no less than three planets coasting along in your sign you're irresistible. You'll find ways of generating extra cash, but this won't necessarily have anything to do with, say, horse racing I'm glad to say. As soon as the opportunity arrives you'll recognize it almost immediately and will act accordingly. Many of you will be signing financial documents, or travelling for the sake of cash matters. In which case you've certainly picked an ideal time for doing just that. Have faith in yourself this month and you won't regret it.

During September, the optimism of August will overlap and initially you will continue to believe that you can afford literally anything. It's only later when your bank account becomes mysteriously empty that you'll wonder whether you had taken leave of your senses, and the answer to that is probably 'yes'. However, there is a chance of taking a short trip which will help to swell the bank account and any documents you sign at this time will also improve your financial position. Make sure, too, that you listen to the ideas of other people even if you don't act upon them, because amongst them is likely to be a money spinner.

Up until 18 October you seem to be spending either on your home or perhaps entertaining, and thoroughly enjoying the experience. However, be warned that after this date Mercury moves into retrograde action, and so anything connected with financial paperwork or travel, will be unbelievably complicated and you may finish up this month all the poorer.

November finds Mercury squatting in the area of property or the home. Therefore, some of you may be moving from one area to another and, spending on furnishing or perhaps solicitors. For others it's a time when you may decide to invite friends back to your house, which you will find difficult to do in a modest fashion; not for you a quick hamburger and a cold salad. Oh no, it's down to the butcher for the best cut of meat, Chinese fruit and lots of goodies for dessert. This is a charming side of your character, that you do love to give, but you must remember there is always a time for that and that time is when you are in funds, which you may not be during this particular month. Don't forget that Christmas isn't too far away and you know how much money you spend during that particular period.

Lastly, December and during this month no one can realistically expect you to play the miser, it just simply isn't your style. The placing of Mercury seems to suggest you are out attending parties, social occasions and doing your best to meet other people whenever you can. It's all very charming, Leo, but do your sums and make sure you have enough money, the sort of money that you won't miss at a later date. If you are totally broke, then the ideal thing to do would be to make your excuses and simply draw in your horns, but this isn't Leo style, you've far too much pride. Naturally, if you are a parent I'm not suggesting you should deny your children, but cut down the number of other gifts you buy in order to impress those at work. Instead, just send them an expensive card, after all, you may quickly discover most other people don't even bother with that.

No one is ever going to completely control a Leo when it comes to cash matters, but you can control yourself. So use the *Monthly* and *Daily Guides* to help you keep your feet on the ground.

Love and Sex Year

WELL LEO, OF THERE'S ONE SIDE OF LIFE you really enjoy, regardless of age, it is love and sex. Many of you are just as interested at 90 as you were at 19. But, of course, for you it's got to be romance, shared secrets and how you remember the feelings of first love. You love to dramatize your fantasies and everything that happens to you because you adore romance.

Even the most ambitious Lion can't be without love and romance, certainly not all the time. It's absolutely nothing to do with loneliness, it's far more complicated than that. While some signs claim they are what they eat, you believe you are what you attract. If unfortunately, it should occur that you're not attracting, you often create a dream world to hide from what you don't want to see. Naturally, disillusionment colours fantasy and then you retreat. However, when this occurs you become rather embittered, or throw yourself into as many projects as you possibly can in order to ease the pain. But luckily, you don't remember the negative sides of life for very long and in no time at all you're back into the swing of things, hoping to find that special someone in order to make life really worthwhile.

Yes, you're one person who desperately needs love,

though you may not always admit it. Sometimes, during certain periods, you flit from one relationship to the next in an effort to hide your insecurity. However, you are a loving and generous sign with plenty of warm qualities which make you lovable. You have great potential for joyful experiences. But when Leo seeks to deceive the emotional self, the price is that life somehow becomes harsh. So what about the year ahead?

During January, you're at your most happy-go-lucky, well up until the 24th anyway. You're keeping those New Year celebrations going for as long as possible, especially if you are without a partner. You're hoping to meet someone in your social whirl and you probably will. But be warned, to enjoy the attentions of the opposite sex is fine but to start whistling the Wedding March after two weeks could make you unpopular.

February will find you strongly attracted to those who come from completely different backgrounds, especially if they have interesting accents. For some there is the chance that if you are involved in any kind of further education then it is there you will find admirers. You'll notice I'm talking in the plural, because I'm afraid you're unlikely to meet anyone that special. Still, at least you will have plenty of friends about, so you're not going to be feeling lonely that's for sure.

During March, there may still be one or two brief encounters with people who come from different backgrounds, or perhaps with those who are involved in higher education. This, of course, needs conscious controlling if you happen to have a partner already, otherwise you're going to find yourself in hot water in no uncertain fashion, especially as Mercury is in retrograde action up until the 13th. Some of you may come across interesting prospects amongst your work colleagues. This is not going to lead to a great affair, so don't over-dramatize it, simply be grateful that you've plenty of company and plenty of invitations for fun.

In April sexual possibilities are likely to come while learning a new skill or perhaps in the company of people who come from different countries. In some instances this could lead to true love, assuming you can be bothered to hang around long enough to see what develops. But if you already have someone, you are likely to find yourself severely admonished, which is the worst thing to do because it will cause you to rebel and become more outrageous. Nevertheless, this can be a fun month and you may even find romance at work. In fact, you can probably find it anywhere, assuming you have your eyes wide open.

The tendency to concentrate on work continues into May, well up until the 20th. Therefore, this is likely to be a rather quiet time for romantic matters unless you can find somebody while you go about your everyday business. If you're single, it might be a good idea to combine business with pleasure whenever possible, but even so don't expect too much. However, friends are likely to be making some interesting introductions. The faces that come from this direction may set your hormones racing, but they're going to leave that heart relatively intact. A month for a great deal of fun but nothing more long-lasting.

June brings possibilities to visit clubs when in the company of friends. What starts off as a casual sex affair, or just a strong attraction, will over the coming weeks develop into something more important. Mind you, if you already have a partner, I'm afraid you're going to find yourself in several sticky situations. You seem to be having a difficult time controlling either your sexual appetite or your emotions at this time. Try explaining that to your loved one and I don't think you'll get very far. Finally, with your money planet in retrograde action, on no account should you attempt to impress other people by spending money, because you will finish up lonely and broke.

During the first 13 days of July you really must be careful, because even if you already have someone you're likely to be sneaking off for several quick affairs with people you hardly know. Ask yourself if this is wise. Certainly from the 13th onwards your social life will be providing you with lots of chances to enjoy yourself. This doesn't necessarily mean you're going to be meeting the 'love of your life', but if you can take these flirtations in the spirit that they are meant, then there's no reason why July can't be a thoroughly enjoyable time.

Of course, August is your month so all of your talents and gifts, both physical and mental, are obvious to everyone and you're likely to gather a crowd. Make sure then that you're relatively picky. There's a tendency here for you to spend in order to impress other people, but underneath you know that anyone who falls for this isn't worth knowing. There's plenty of chances for fun and socializing, and while at parties you may meet interesting members of the opposite sex. However, if you are attached it could be quite a troublesome time, so exercise some control. I'm not going to tell you what to do, because the choice is entirely yours.

When it comes to romance, September is a quiet month, unless you meet somebody while going about your job. Of course, if you've already got someone, this won't worry you one little bit. For some there seem to be reasons why you need to give attention to property and family matters, perhaps there's some kind of drama or tension going on there. This may require your charm and conciliatory powers. So, you single Lions must not expect to meet the man or woman of your dreams this month.

October socially and sexually is a little quiet up until the 19th, but once Venus enters the fiery sign of Sagittarius everything seems to break loose. You appear to be finding admirers everywhere you go, and you're a bit like a child in a sweet shop. This, of course, can be highly dangerous if you are supposed to be in love. In which case the relationship may be broken off unless you're very careful. However, if this doesn't apply, enjoy yourself, always taking the necessary precautions of course. Also, remember it isn't always necessary to turn the romantic side of life into a big film even though that is your general attitude.

You should exercise a certain amount of caution in November. Certainly, there's chance from the 13th onwards that you may become involved with somebody you meet through your job. But this is a simple flirtation rather than anything world shattering. However, what really needs watching is the fact that Mars will be in the sign of Libra, so those hormones of yours are leaping about. You are likely to become temporarily involved with the most unsuitable people, simply for the sake of satisfying that animal appetite of yours. If you're not careful you may look back on this month and wonder what on earth had come over you. You may have reasons for regret, because one admirer may simply not let go and could become quite obsessive to the point where you may have to lose that charming exterior of yours and turn on the acid.

Lastly, December, and a better month of the year mainly due to the fact that Venus is in your opposite sign of Aquarius. So if you're already in a relationship you may decide on a Christmas wedding. If not, accept all those invitations because though you may encounter mostly flirting there's likely to be somebody who is really worthwhile and the trick is not to miss them. December always brings out the romantic in all of us and in your case it could really lead to something. Make sure you're looking your best at all times and, above all else, keep your eyes open.

Health and Diet Year

YOUR SIGN RULES THE VERTEBRAE, diaphragm and calf muscles, and the aorta, anterior and the posterior coronary arteries. And just one organ, but the most important one, the heart. Any form of heart ailments fall under this sign's domain. Leo can be also responsible for back ailments of many varieties, in a kind of reflex action to Aquarius which is your opposite sign. Because you are vulnerable to back ailments, posture is extremely important, and so if it is necessary for you to sit at a desk for any length of time and you begin to feel problems in these areas, find an excuse to get up and walk around for a while.

You need to pay attention to what you eat too. The following foods are particularly valuable for the average Lion: sugar beet, oats, cocoa, savoy cabbage, oranges, lemons and lettuce, plums (which are rich in magnesium and can help to relieve complaints due to excess acid), wheatbran (which provides roughage) and peas (which help the body to remove acid deposits).

In general, you are a healthy, robust person and have a horror of being sick. Being caged up and physically incapacitated gets you into a panic. Since everything you need and desire is dependent on your ability to move about, life is not worth living if you have to spend it in bed alone. Well, what about your health during the year ahead?

There are going to be two areas during January that need watching because of the placing of Mars in Pisces. It's possible that too much worry will bring on headaches due to thoughtlessness and minor mishaps. Mind you, Venus' position in Sagittarius until the 24th will certainly be livening up your social life, so hangovers and overeating are other areas which need to be carefully watched.

February finds Mars in the long-distance travelling part of your chart. Therefore, if you're visiting different climates and eating unusual food that your tummy is not used to, you are advised to take it easy, otherwise you may find yourself laid up and missing out on all of the fun. A little bit of preventive action, though, can save you a great deal of trouble.

There's precious little danger for you during March, unless you happen to be in a foreign country. In which case up until the 22nd food poisoning or minor cuts and burns are a distinct possibility. However, as you usually keep your mind on what you are doing, you may just be able to escape this tiny pitfall. In order to find out more read the *Monthly* and *Daily Guides*.

During April, you may discover that arguments with acquaintances and friends may upset your equilibrium. But before you act try to stay calm and make an effort to understand what they're getting at. I'm quite certain that they don't mean to upset you, but right now you're in a hypersensitive mood.

If anything's going to lay you low during May, it's going to be hard work. You seem to have lost all sense of proportion and for the most part are ignoring the big wide world, even though there are chances to have fun in connection with work colleagues. Do yourself a big favour, make sure that you get out and let off steam at least once a week. This will ensure that you stay hale and hearty. Also, a good deal of love, of course, always helps. There's no one happier than the Lion who is being stroked and petted.

During June, there may be some frustration if you are travelling, which will get on your nerves but it won't be anything too serious. However, disagreements at work could also make those nerves jangle. Although this is unlikely to last for very long, it may do equal damage if you go out and celebrate the end of your differences.

Venus is in your sign during July and so you're physically and mentally looking and feeling great. The only trouble is that you will be attracted to rich food and late nights. But if you can keep a sense of proportion, you should have no difficulty whatsoever.

August is, of course, your month and you've plenty of energy which is radiating from every pore. What's more the only problem is that too much of a good thing may bring minor complaints, but nothing that will keep you awake at night.

September sees you obsessed by money affairs, which you may lose sleep over and wake up the next day feeling extremely bad-tempered. Arguments with other people could add to your stress, so keep a sense of proportion and realize that everybody is entitled to their opinion.

During October, there seems to be a great deal of activity going on at home, but none of which you seem to be enjoying. As a kind-hearted person who generally likes to please other people, you often put your own needs second. I'm not suggesting that you suddenly become selfish, but if somebody else is hogging the limelight and bossing you around, then it might be a good idea to sit down and have a talk. They can then see the error of their ways and you'll stay in good health.

November is one of the most difficult times of the year for trying to buy property and sorting out family affairs. Both could give you a major headache. This in turn leads to a certain amount of stress. But counter this by sticking to a sensible diet and making sure that you rest up – perhaps on your own for a change.

Of course there's not much hope for any of us in December, regardless of our star sign. We all have good intentions about eating sensibly and not overdoing the alcohol, but they fly out of the window once the festive period actually arrives. To make matters worse, you seem to be rather accident prone at home, particularly in the kitchen with hot and sharp objects. Therefore, if you are preparing the Christmas dinner, don't allow other people to harass or rush you. Take things slowly and in your own good time and you will end this year in your usual healthy state.

Numerology Year

IN ORDER TO DISCOVER the number of any year you are interested in, your 'individual year number', first take your birth date, day and month, and add this to the year you are interested in, be it in the past or in the future. As an example, say you were born on 13 September and you are interested in the year 2001:

$$
\begin{array}{r}
13 \\
9 \\
2001 \\
\hline
2023
\end{array}
$$

Then, write down 2 + 0 + 2 + 3 and you will discover this equals 7. This means that the number of your year is 7. If the number adds up to more than 9, add these two digits together.

You can experiment with this method by taking any year from your past and following this guide to find whether or not numerology works out for you.

The guide is perennial and applicable to all Sun signs: you can look up years for your friends as well as for yourself. Use it to discover general trends ahead,

Numerology Year

the way you should be approaching a chosen period and how you can make the most of the future.

Individual Year Number 1

General Feel
A time for being more self-sufficient and one when you should be ready to grasp the nettle. All opportunities must be snapped up, after careful consideration. Also an excellent time for laying down the foundations for future success in all areas.

Definition
Because this is the number 1 individual year, you will have the chance to start again in many areas of life. The emphasis will be upon the new; there will be fresh faces in your life, more opportunities and perhaps even new experiences. If you were born on either the 1st, 19th or 28th and were born under the sign of Aries or Leo then this will be an extremely important time. It is crucial during this cycle that you be prepared to go it alone, push back horizons and generally open up your mind. Time also for playing the leader or pioneer wherever necessary. If you have a hobby which you wish to turn into a business, or maybe you simply wish to introduce other people to your ideas and plans, then do so whilst experiencing this individual cycle. A great period too for laying down the plans for long-term future gains. Therefore, make sure you do your homework well and you will reap the rewards at a later date.

Relationships

This is an ideal period for forming new bonds, perhaps business relationships, new friends and new loves too. You will be attracted to those in high positions and with strong personalities. There may also be an emphasis on bonding with people a good deal younger than yourself. If you are already in a long-standing relationship, then it is time to clear away the dead wood between you which may have been causing misunderstandings and unhappiness. Whether in love or business, you will find those who were born under the sign of Aries, Leo or Aquarius far more common in your life, also those born on the following dates: 1st, 4th, 9th, 10th, 13th, 18th, 19th, 22nd and 28th. The most important months for this individual year, when you are likely to meet up with those who have a strong influence on you, are January, May, July and October.

Career

It is likely that you have been wanting to break free and to explore fresh horizons in your job or in your career and this is definitely a year for doing so. Because you are in a fighting mood, and because your decision-making qualities as well as your leadership qualities are foremost, it will be an easy matter for you to find assistance as well as to impress other people. Major professional changes are likely and you will also feel more independent within your existing job. Should you want times for making important career moves, then choose Mondays or Tuesdays. These are good days for pushing your luck and presenting your ideas well. Changes connected with your career are going to be more likely during April, May, July and September.

Health

If you have forgotten the name of your doctor or dentist, then this is the year for going for check-ups. A time too when people of a certain age are likely to start wearing glasses. The emphasis seems to be on the eyes. Start a good health regime. This will help you cope with any adverse events that almost assuredly lie ahead. The important months for your own health as well as for loved ones are March, May and August.

Individual Year Number 2

General Feel
You will find it far easier to relate to other people.

Definition
What you will need during this cycle is diplomacy, cooperation and the ability to put yourself in someone else's shoes. Whatever you began last year will now begin to show signs of progress. However, don't expect miracles; changes are going to be slow rather than at the speed of light. Changes will be taking place all around you. It is possible too that you will be considering moving from one area to another, maybe even to another country. There is a lively feel about domesticity and in relationships with the opposite sex, too. This is going to be a marvellous year for making things come true and asking for favours. However, on no account should you force yourself and your opinions on other people. A spoonful of honey is

going to get you a good deal further than a spoonful of vinegar. If you are born under the sign of Cancer or Taurus, or if your birthday falls on the 2nd, 11th, 20th or 29th, then this year is going to be full of major events.

Relationships

You need to associate with other people far more than is usually the case – perhaps out of necessity. The emphasis is on love, friendship and professional partnerships. The opposite sex will be much more prepared to get involved in your life than is normally the case. This is a year your chances of becoming engaged or married are increased and there is likely to be an increase in your family in the form of a lovely addition and also in the families of your friends and those closest to you. The instinctive and caring side to your personality is going to be strong and very obvious. You will quickly discover that you will be particularly touchy and sensitive to things that other people say. Further, you will find those born under the sign of Cancer, Taurus and Libra entering your life far more than is usually the case. This also applies to those who were born on the 2nd, 6th, 7th, 11th, 15th, 20th, 24th, 25th or 29th of the month.

Romantic and family events are likely to be emphasized during April, June and September.

Career

There is a strong theme of change here, but there is no point in having a panic attack about that because, after all, life is about change. However, in this particular individual year any transformation or upheaval is likely to be of an internal nature, such as at your place of work, rather than external. You may find your company is moving from one area to another, or perhaps there are changes between departments. Quite obviously then, the most important thing for you to do in order to make your life easy is to be adaptable. There is a strong possibility, too, that you may be given added responsibility. Do not flinch as this will bring in extra reward.

If you are thinking of searching for employment this year, then try to arrange all meetings and negotiations on Monday and Friday. These are good days for asking for favours or rises too. The best months are March, April, June, August, and December. All these are important times for change.

Health

This individual cycle emphasizes stomach problems. The important thing for you is to eat sensibly, rather than go on, for example, a crash diet – this could be detrimental. If you are female then you would be wise to have a check-up at least once during the year ahead just to be sure you can continue to enjoy good health. All should be discriminating when dining out. Check cutlery, and take care if food has only been partially cooked. Furthermore, emotional stress could get you down, but only if you allow it. Provided you set aside some periods of relaxation in each day when you can close your eyes and let everything drift away, then you will have little to worry about. When it comes to diet, be sure that the emphasis is on nutrition, rather than fighting the flab. Perhaps it would be a good idea to become less weight conscious during this period and let your body find its natural ideal weight on its own. The months of February, April, July and November may show health changes in some way. Common sense is your best guide during this year.

Individual Year Number 3

General Feel
You are going to be at your most creative and imaginative during this time. There is a theme of expansion and growth and you will want to polish up your self-image in order to make the 'big impression'.

Definition
It is a good year for reaching out, for expansion. Social and artistic developments should be interesting as well as profitable and this will help to promote happiness. There will be a strong urge in you to improve yourself, either your image or your reputation or perhaps your mind. Your popularity soars through the ceiling and this delights you. Involving yourself with something creative brings increased success plus a good deal of satisfaction. However, it is imperative that you keep yourself in a positive mood. This will attract attention and appreciation of all of your talents. Projects which were begun two years ago are likely to be bearing fruit this year. If you were born under the sign of Pisces or Sagittarius, or your birthday falls on the 3rd, 12th, 21st or 30th, then this year is going to be particularly special and successful.

Relationships

There is a happy-go-lucky feel about all your relationships and you are in a flirty, fancy-free mood. Heaven help anyone trying to catch you during the next twelve months: they will need to get their skates on. Relationships are likely to be light-hearted and fun rather than heavy going. It is possible too that you will find yourself with those who are younger than you, particularly those born under the signs of Pisces and Sagittarius, and those whose birth dates add up to 3, 6 or 9. Your individual cycle shows important months for relationships are March, May, August and December.

Career

As I discussed earlier, this individual number is one that suggests branching out and personal growth, so be ready to take on anything new. Not surprisingly, your career aspects look bright and shiny. You are definitely going to be more ambitious and must keep up that positive façade and attract opportunities. Avoid taking obligations too lightly; it is important that you adopt a conscientious approach to all your responsibilities. You may take on a fresh course of learning or look for a new job, and the important days for doing so would be on Thursday and Friday: these are definitely your best days. This is particularly true in the months of February, March, May, July and November: expect expansion in your life and take a chance during these times.

Health

Because you are likely to be out and about painting the town all the colours of the rainbow, it is likely that health problems could come through over-indulgence or perhaps tiredness. However, if you have got to have some health problems, I suppose these are the best ones to experience, because they are under your control. There is also a possibility that you may get a little fraught over work, which may result in some emotional scenes. However, you are sensible enough to realize they should not be taken too seriously. If you are prone to skin allergies, then these too could be giving you problems during this particular year. The best advice you can follow is not to go to extremes that will affect your body or your mind. It is all very well to have fun, but after a while too much of it not only affects your health but also the degree of enjoyment you experience. Take extra care between January and March, and June and October, especially where these are winter months for you.

Individual Year Number 4

General Feel
It is back to basics this year. Do not build on shaky foundations. Get yourself organized and be prepared to work a little harder than you usually do and you will come through without any great difficulty.

Definition
It is imperative this year that you have a grand plan. Do not simply rush off without considering the consequences and avoid dabbling of any kind. It is likely, too, that you will be gathering more responsibility and

on occasions this could lead you to feeling unappreciated, claustrophobic and perhaps over-burdened in some ways. Although it is true to say that this cycle in your individual life tends to bring about a certain amount of limitation, whether this be on the personal side to life, the psychological or the financial, you now have the chance to get yourself together and to build on more solid foundations. Security is definitely your key word at this time. When it comes to any project, job or plan, it is important that you ask the right questions. In other words, do your homework before you go off half-cock. That would be a disaster. If you are an Aquarius, a Leo or a Gemini or you were born on the 4th, 13th, 22nd, or the 31st of any month, this individual year will be extremely important and long remembered.

Relationships

You will find that it is the eccentric, the unusual, the unconventional and the downright odd that will be drawn into your life during this particular cycle. It is also strongly possible that people you have not met for some time may be re-entering your circle and an older person or somebody outside your own social or perhaps religious background will be drawn to you, too. When it comes to the romantic side of life, again you are drawn to that which is different from usual. You may even form a relationship with someone who comes from a totally different background, perhaps from far away. Something unusual about them stimulates and excites you. Gemini, Leo and Aquarius are your likely favourites, as well as anyone whose birth number adds up to 1, 4, 5, or 7. Certainly, the most exciting months for romance are going to be February, April, July and November. Make sure then that you socialize a lot during this particular time, and be ready for literally anything.

Career

Once more we have the theme of the unusual and different in this area of life. You may be plodding along in the same old rut when suddenly lightning strikes and you find yourself besieged by offers from other people and, in a panic, not quite sure what to do. There may be a period when nothing particular seems to be going on, when, to your astonishment, you are given a promotion or some exciting challenge. Literally anything can happen in this particular cycle of your life. The individual year 4 also inclines towards added responsibilities and it is important that you do not offload them onto other people or cringe in fear. They will eventually pay off and in the meantime you will be gaining in experience and paving the way for greater success in the future. When you want to arrange any kind of meeting, negotiation or perhaps ask for a favour at work, then try to do so on a Monday or a Wednesday for the luckiest results. January, February, April, October and November are certainly the months when you must play the opportunist and be ready to say yes to anything that comes your way.

Health

The biggest problems that you will have to face this year are caused by stress, so it is important that you attend to your diet and take life as philosophically as possible, as well as being ready to adapt to changing conditions. You are likely to find that people you thought you knew well are acting out of character and this throws you off balance. Take care, too, when visiting the doctor. Remember that you are dealing with a human being and that doctors, like the rest of us, can make mistakes. Unless you are 100 per cent satisfied then go for a second opinion over anything important. Try to be sceptical about yourself because you are going to be a good deal more moody than usual. The times that need special attention are February, May, September and November. If any of these months fall in the winter part of your year, then wrap up well and dose up on vitamin C.

Individual Year Number 5

General Feel
There will be many more opportunities for you to get out and about and travel is certainly going to be playing a large part in your year. Change too must be expected and even embraced – after all, it is part of life. You will have more free time and choices, so all in all things look promising.

Definition
It is possible that you tried previously to get something off the launching pad, but for one reason or another it simply didn't happen. Luckily, you now get a chance to renew those old plans and put them into action. You are certainly going to feel that things are changing for the better in all areas. You are going to be more actively involved with the public and will enjoy a certain amount

of attention and publicity. You may have failed in the past but this year mistakes will be easier to accept and learn from; you are going to find yourself both physically and mentally more in tune with your environment and with those you care about than ever before. If you are a Gemini or a Virgo or were born on the 5th, 14th or 23rd then this is going to be a period of major importance for you and you must be ready to take advantage of this.

Relationships

Lucky you! Your sexual magnetism goes through the ceiling and you will be involved in many relationships during the year ahead. You have that extra charisma about you which will be attracting others and you can look forward to being choosy. There will be an inclination to be drawn to those who are considerably younger than yourself. It is likely too that you will find that those born under the signs of Taurus, Gemini, Virgo and Libra as well as those whose birth date adds up to 2, 5 or 6 will play an important part in your year. The months for attracting others in a big way are January, March, June, October and December.

Career

This is considered by all numerologists as being one of the best numbers for self-improvement in all areas, but particularly on the professional front. It will be relatively easy for you to sell your ideas and yourself, as well as to push your skills and expertise under the noses of other people. They will certainly sit up and take notice. Clearly, then, a time for you to view the world as your oyster and to get out there and grab your piece of the action. You have increased confidence and should be able to get exactly what you want. Friday and Wednesday

Numerology Year

are perhaps the best days if looking for a job or going to negotiations or interviews, or in fact for generally pushing yourself into the limelight. Watch out for March, May, September, October or December. Something of great importance could pop up at this time. There will certainly be a chance for advancement; whether you take it or not is, of course, entirely up to you.

Health

Getting a good night's rest could be your problem during the year ahead, since that mind of yours is positively buzzing and won't let you rest. Try turning your brain off at bedtime, otherwise you will finish up irritable and exhausted. Try to take things a step at a time without rushing around. Meditation may help you to relax and do more for your physical wellbeing than anything else. Because this is an extremely active year, you will need to do some careful planning so that you can cope with ease rather than rushing around like a demented may-fly. Furthermore, try to avoid going over the top with alcohol, food, sex, gambling or anything which could be described as 'get rich quick'. During January, April, August, and October, watch yourself a bit, you could do with some coddling, particularly if these happen to be winter months for you.

Individual Year Number 6

General Feel

There is likely to be increased responsibility and activity within your domestic life. There will be many occasions when you will be helping loved ones and your sense of duty is going to be strong.

Definition

Activities for the most part are likely to be centred around property, family, loved ones, romance and your home. Your artistic appreciation will be good and you will be drawn to anything that is colourful and beautiful, and possessions that have a strong appeal to your eye or even your ear. Where domesticity is concerned, there is a strong suggestion that you may move out of one home into another. This is an excellent time too for self-education, for branching out, for graduating, for taking on some extra courses – whether simply to improve your appearance or to improve your mind. When it comes to your social life you are inundated with chances to attend events. You are going to be a real social butterfly, flitting from scene to scene and enjoying yourself thoroughly. Try to accept nine out of ten invitations that come your way because they bring with them chances of advancement. If you were born on the 6th, 15th or 24th or should your birth sign be Taurus, Libra or Cancer then this is going to be a year that will be long remembered as a very positive one.

Relationships

When it comes to love, sex and romance the individual year 6 is perhaps the most successful. It is a time for being swept off your feet, for becoming engaged or even getting married. On the more negative side, perhaps there is a separation and divorce. However, the latter can be avoided, provided you are prepared to sit down and communicate properly. There is an emphasis too on pregnancy and birth, or changes in existing relationships. Circumstances will be sweeping you along. If you are born under the sign of Taurus, Cancer or Libra, then it is even more likely that this will be a major year for you, as well as for those born on dates adding up to 6, 3 or 2. The most memorable months of your year are going to be February, May, September and November. Grab all opportunities to enjoy yourself and improve your relationships during these periods.

Career

A good year for this side to life too, with the chances of promotion and recognition for past efforts all coming your way. You will be able to improve your position in life even though it is likely that recently you have been disappointed. On the cash front, big rewards will come flooding in mainly because you are prepared to fulfil your obligations and commitments without complaint or protest. Other people will appreciate all the efforts you have put in, so plod along and you will find your efforts will not have been in vain. Perversely, if you are looking for a job or setting up an interview, negotiation or a meeting, or simply want to advertise your talents in some way, then your best days for doing so are Monday, Thursday and Friday. Long-term opportunities are very strong during the months of February, April, August, September and November. These are the key periods for pushing yourself up the ladder of success.

Health

If you are to experience any problems of a physical nature during this year, then they could be tied up with the throat, nose or the tonsils plus the upper parts of the body. Basically, what you need to stay healthy during this year is plenty of sunlight, moderate exercise, fresh air and changes of scene. Escape to the coast if this is at all possible. The months for being particularly watchful are March, July, September and December. Think twice before doing anything during these times and there is no reason why you shouldn't stay hale and hearty for the whole year.

Individual Year Number 7

General Feel

A year for inner growth and for finding out what really makes you tick and what you need to make you happy. Self-awareness and discovery are all emphasized during the individual year 7.

Definition

You will be provided with the opportunity to place as much emphasis as possible on your personal life and your own wellbeing. There will be many occasions when you will find yourself analysing your past motives and actions, and giving more attention to your own personal needs, goals and desires. There will also be many occasions when you will want to escape any kind of confusion, muddle or noise; time spent alone will not

Numerology Year

be wasted. This will give you the chance to meditate and also to examine exactly where you have come to so far, and where you want to go in the future. It is important you make up your mind what you want out of this particular year because once you have done so you will attain those ambitions. Failure to do this could mean you end up chasing your own tail and that is a pure waste of time and energy. You will also discover that secrets about yourself and other people could be surfacing during this year. If you were born under the sign of Pisces or Cancer, or on the 7th, 16th or 25th of the month, then this year will be especially wonderful.

Relationships

It has to be said from the word go that this is not the best year for romantic interest. A strong need for contemplation will mean spending time on your own. Any romance that does develop this year may not live up to your expectations, but, providing you are prepared to take things as they come without jumping to conclusions, then you will enjoy yourself without getting hurt. Decide exactly what it is you have in mind and then go for it. Romantic interests this year are likely to be with people who were born on dates that add up to 2, 4 or 7 or with people born under the sign of Cancer or Pisces. Watch for romantic opportunities during January, April, August and October.

Career

When we pass through this particular individual cycle, two things in life tend to occur: retirement from the limelight, and a general slowing down, perhaps by taking leave of absence or maybe retraining in some way. It is likely too that you will become more aware of your own occupational expertise and skills – you will begin to understand your true purpose in life and will feel much more enlightened. Long-sought-after goals begin to come to life if you have been drifting of late. The best attitude to have throughout this year is an exploratory one when it comes to your work. If you want to set up negotiations, interviews or meetings, arrange them for Monday or Friday. In fact, any favours you seek should be tackled on these days. January, March, July, August, October and December are particularly good for self-advancement.

Health

Since, in comparison to previous years, this is a rather quiet time, health problems are likely to be minor. Some will possibly come through irritation or worry and the best thing to do is to attempt to remain meditative and calm. This state of mind will bring positive results. Failure to do so may create unnecessary problems by allowing your imagination to run completely out of control. You need time this year to restore, recuperate and contemplate. Any health changes that do occur are likely to happen in February, June, August and November.

Individual Year Number 8

General Feel

This is going to be a time for success, for making important moves and changes, a time when you may gain

Numerology Year

power and certainly one when your talents are going to be recognized.

Definition

This individual year gives you the chance to 'think big'; it is a time when you can occupy the limelight and wield power. If you were born on the 8th, 17th or 26th of the month or come under the sign of Capricorn, pay attention to this year and make sure you make the most of it. You should develop greater maturity and discover a true feeling of faith and destiny, both in yourself and in events that occur. This part of the cycle is connected with career, ambition and money, but debts from the past will have to be repaid. For example, an old responsibility or debt that you may have avoided in past years may reappear to haunt you. However, whatever you do with these twelve months, aim high – think big, think success and above all be positive.

Relationships

This particular individual year is one which is strongly connected with birth, divorce and marriage – most of the landmarks we experience in life, in fact. Lovewise, those who are more experienced or older than you, or people of power, authority, influence or wealth will be very attractive. This year will be putting you back in touch with those from your past – old friends, comrades, associates, and even romances from long ago crop up once more. You should not experience any great problems romantically this year, especially if you are dealing with Capricorns or Librans, or with those whose date of birth adds up to 8, 6 or 3. The best months for romance to develop are likely to be March, July, September and December.

Career
The number 8 year is generally believed to be the best one when it comes to bringing in cash. It is also good for asking for a rise or achieving promotion or authority over other people. This is your year for basking in the limelight of success, the result perhaps of your past efforts. Now you will be rewarded. Financial success is all but guaranteed, provided you keep faith with your ambitions and yourself. It is important that you set major goals for yourself and work slowly towards them. You will be surprised how easily they are fulfilled. Conversely, if you are looking for work, then do set up interviews, negotiations and meetings, preferably on Saturday, Thursday or Friday, which are your luckiest days. Also watch out for chances to do yourself a bit of good during February, June, July, September and November.

Health
You can avoid most health problems, particularly headaches, constipation or liver problems, by avoiding depression and feelings of loneliness. It is important when these descend that you keep yourself busy enough not to dwell on them. When it comes to receiving attention from the medical profession you would be well advised to get a second opinion. Eat wisely, try to keep a positive and enthusiastic outlook on life and all will be well. Periods which need special care are January, May, July and October. Therefore, if these months fall during the winter part of your year, wrap up well and dose yourself with vitamins.

Individual Year Number 9

General Feel
A time for tying up loose ends. Wishes are likely to be fulfilled and matters brought to swift conclusions. Inspiration runs amok. Much travel is likely.

Definition
The number 9 individual year is perhaps the most successful of all. It tends to represent the completion of matters and affairs, whether in work, business, or personal affairs. Your ability to let go of habits, people and negative circumstances or situations, that may have been holding you back, is strong. The sympathetic and humane side to your character also surfaces and you learn to give more freely of yourself without expecting anything in return. Any good deeds that you do will certainly be well rewarded, in terms of satisfaction and perhaps financially too. If you were born under the sign of Aries or Scorpio, or on the 9th, 18th or 27th of the month, this is certainly going to be an all-important year.

Relationships
The individual year 9 is a cycle which gives appeal as well as influence. Because of this, you will be getting emotionally tied up with members of the opposite sex who may be outside your usual cultural or ethnic group. The reason for this is that this particular number relates to humanity and, of course, this tends to quash ignorance, pride and bigotry. You also discover that Aries, Leo and Scorpio people are going to be much more evident in your domestic affairs, as well as those whose birth dates add

up to 9, 3 or 1. The important months for relationships are February, June, August and November. These will be extremely hectic and eventful from a romantic viewpoint and there are times when you could be swept off your feet.

Career

This is a year which will help to make many of your dreams and ambitions come true. Furthermore, it is an excellent time for success if you are involved in marketing your skills, talents and expertise more widely. You may be thinking of expanding abroad for example and, if so, this is certainly a good idea. You will find that harmony and cooperation with your fellow workers are easier than before and this will help your dreams and ambitions. The best days for you if you want to line up meetings or negotiations are going to be Tuesday and Thursday and this also applies if you are looking for employment or want a special day for doing something of an ambitious nature. Employment or business changes could also feature during January, May, June, August and October.

Health

The only physical problems you may have during this particular year will be because of accidents, so be careful. Try too to avoid unnecessary tension and arguments with other people. Take extra care when you are on the roads: no drinking and driving for example. You will only have problems if you play your own worst enemy. Be extra careful when in the kitchen or bathroom: sharp instruments that you find in these areas can lead to cuts, unless you take care.

Your Sun Sign Partner

Leo with Leo

A LEO WITH A LEO SPELLS EITHER love or hate, sometimes both. Competition can trail off to the truly absurd as he explains to her the principle of nuclear fission, while she, a doctor of physics, fulminates into a fiery explosion. He is horrified that she can't appreciate his helpfulness, and lets her know that she belongs in a zoo.

Should the smoke be dispersed by sheer chemistry, this combination has potential because both share the same values, sense of romance and materialistic attitudes. When she invites him to dinner, he gasps at the mousse, sighs at the wine and moans with delight over the baked Alaska. In turn, he nourishes her femininity with fresh flowers and remembers to tell her she looks beautiful by candlelight.

Leo Woman

Leo woman with Aries man

This is nothing less than love at first sight, when he dashes aggressively to her side to retrieve the diary she deliberately drops. He is quick to pick up her cues and be complimentary, especially when she lets her eyes drift. He adores the challenge of winning her, and her flirtations give him many challenges. The problem is that his flirtations give her indigestion. She can't imagine why he would even consider glancing at that blonde slinking by when she is right there. This is a man who can make hearts beat faster, and she is a woman who can make his stop dead. Between them there is much excitement, communication and kisses, not to mention a few airborne objects.

Leo woman with Taurus man

This is definitely not a match made in heaven, as they both have a will that could topple a redwood tree. He is stubborn and rigid; she is defiant and stubborn. Combined, these inharmonious qualities spell trouble. He is a stay-at-home, while she walks holes in the floor if she can't get out. She likes the drama and excitement of life, he is content with the 10 o'clock news.

It's a mystery what even brought these two together. As to the outcome of this strange and stormy combination, even the stars avoid any responsibility.

Leo woman with Gemini man

He'll charm his way in and out of her life so fast she'll forget she ever knew him. Should he stick around, he won't woo her with romantic notions, be on time for the wedding or remember her first name. His charisma comes from the fact that he's so clever. His hang-up is that emotionally he's a fool.

This man is friendly but fickle. His attention moves faster than a speeding bullet, and his thoughts change every second. He's bored unless she beats him at being amusing, which can be a little exhausting unless she works in the entertainment business. If she's fast enough, she might fascinate him for an hour. But then he'll probably walk away while she is still talking.

Leo woman with Cancer man

Although he loves romantic games, the Crab is soon a victim of his own emotions. He has called her 12 times a day and she's still busy. On the first call he's casually interested, by the sixth he's merely impassioned, by the ninth he feverishly abandons all control, but by the thirteenth, he can no longer think and mutters to himself about suicide from overeating.

For even a Leo's sensibilities, his histrionics are indecently excessive. At his most dramatic, the Cancer man is dark, brooding and could easily upset Hamlet, and when his affections are unappeased, he melts into melancholia and defiant doldrums. Only if her love life has been less exciting than a Sunday morning at a convent can she persuade herself into considering Mr Cancer. Chances are that during the weeks of wooing his super-sensitivity will start to strangle her nerve endings.

Leo woman with Virgo man

Despite his bad press as a fussy, nit-picker, who brushes dandruff off her collar, the Virgo man is really not as bad as he sounds. However, he is shy, studious, cautious, introverted and analytical. He loves order and has more systems than an overwrought accountant. She likes the social flurry of dinners, parties, theatre and ballet. He would rather read about them than live them. The cold constrictions of his logic elude her, while the lack of feeling in her histrionics leaves him distraught.

Yet Mr Virgo is kind, loyal and faithful. But unless he has Libra or Leo rising and shares her sense of drama and extravagance, intervals of tedium may be the price they have to pay for such stability.

Leo woman with Libra man

He'll compliment her clothing, send her 17 Valentines and learn to make love without smudging her make-up. This is the man who invented romance, so she shouldn't be surprised when she receives tender telegrams at 10 pm and roses with champagne at midnight. She shares his love of ballet, music and books that no one else has ever heard of. They both love luxury, have a strong sense of beauty and take sugar substitutes with their grapefruit.

Her jealousy is his obvious nemesis and agonizing insecurity follows in its footsteps. She feels like she's a contestant in the Miss World contest and wonders if she'll make the finals or be eliminated. If she wants excitement through sharing, then she probably won't be willing to settle for just a bathing suit contest.

Leo woman with Scorpio man

This combination is passion personified and exciting, but as the emotions appear through the steam just stand back and watch her sanity go up in smoke. He is an enigma, even to himself. But she'll understand him because they're starting from the same place – total obscurity. The key to this man is that he talks in a code: 'I like your ambition; there's a great project I think we could collaborate on.' Meaning: 'I know you don't want to waste any time either, so let's roll down the sheets.' His code is not something he consciously creates every night for the next day's communication. But Mr Scorpio is complex and as strange, bizarre and peculiar as it may be, that's the way his mind works. She's always fantasized about someone strong enough to fearlessly lead her about. Well congratulations, she's found him, but now that fantasy is over she thinks she'll be moving along.

Leo woman with Sagittarius man

She's like putty in his hands, and he knows it. Her smiles and laughter never stop, even when he's not saying anything. His good humour is indicative of his optimism and philosophy of life. She cherishes this and wants to put him in a golden box for a rainy day. The problem is that he must keep moving and sometimes this means moving out of her life. This relationship can be very successful, however, it all depends on her degree of control.

Leo woman with Capricorn man

This man takes everything in life seriously, so if she really wants him she'd better watch her temper. If she smiles sweetly and speaks softly, he'll walk the dog, take out the garbage and forget there are other women in the world. His price for such fidelity is control. Like Mr Leo, this man loves telling her what to do at every waking moment. He was the original model for the male chauvinist pig and his ideas haven't changed very much. His pace will never be as fast as she would like it, but he has stamina. He is, however, strong, sincere, honest and loving. If she's smart she'll shut her mouth and exert her warming influence and then she might even get him to support some of her causes.

Leo woman with Aquarius man

He is the detached humanitarian, while she is the emotional narcissist. His desire is to be friends with the world; her desire is to make sure that the 'world' doesn't include women. At parties he enjoys observing, while she slinks about to see what he's observing. He may find that he's pouring her drink over someone else's sleeve, then his bright-eyed curiosity brings him over to the stunning blonde next to the celery tray. With one unobtrusive giant step forward, she moves in to smilingly distract his attention. When he thinks enough about it, he may decide that she is the best attraction around. Mr Aquarius is not bedazzled by beauty. His ideal is a three-ring circus, and so far she's come the closest. However, will he have the energy to be lion-tamer?

Leo woman with Pisces man

He falls in love fast and sends her skyward with the verbal splendours of a romantic midnight movie. Unfortunately, it's usually a double feature, beginning with something like *Love Story* and ending with *Gone with the Wind*. The younger she is, the better this duo is, because she'll find that all Pisces men seem to use the same emotional orchestrations. She's known few in her lifetime and so she'll be wary, impatient and tell him that she only has time for one side of the record.

At 60, the Pisces man will seek a romance more fabulous than his fantasies. Needless to say, he rarely finds it, and the sad part is that he never stops looking. He embraces an infantile idea of romance and dwells on the memories of his most divine love. He's addicted to her larger-than-life lustre. The problem is that he can't tell the difference between love and addiction. The burden is on her, the blame on him. If she should choose to get involved in his games of emotional monopoly, then she needs to make sure that she is the banker.

LEO MAN

Leo man with Aries woman

If he gets in her way, she'll stand on his feet and ask what he's doing there. He's always liked assertive, active women and she's a dynamo. Her energy level exceeds that of a swarm of angry wasps, and at times he'll have to jog just to keep up with her.

She loves a challenge, so he will inflame her with his flirtations. After she decides she wants him she'll take over and move in so fast that a hurricane would be lethargic by comparison. She's direct and strides the shortest distance between two points. There are moments when his sense of dignity might dissolve under her candour, yet at the same time he'll be pleased that she doesn't take up his time with details.

Leo man with Taurus woman

Miss Taurus is very security conscious, in both material and emotional ways. So he must buy her daffodils, take her to a French restaurant and over the dessert croon 'It Had To Be You'. Suddenly she's his, and even forgets to eat her ice-cream. He should join a health club immediately because she's already started to plan her menus. However, if he is at the point where his jaded soul has seen it all already, then she may just be the woman. Sexually, she's a sensuous animal, but she can exhaust his senses if he's been working nights to prepare for a promotion.

If he loves midnight marathons, seven-course dinners, a loyal, devoted wife, mother and executive housekeeper, then he's on. But some words of warning, he must watch his temper and his flirtation. Next to Scorpio, a Taurus woman is the most jealous and possessive of the signs.

Leo man with Gemini woman

It's a challenge just trying to get her on the telephone, even though she has two. After he's torn his out of the wall because he can't stand the incessant busy signal, he will charge round to her door just in time to see two angry men coming out. She'll run his ego through the wringer and in a very amiable way. He'll never know where she's coming from or where she's going, but then neither does she. She loves novelty, so he must create his own carnival. She loathes commitment, so he must be debonair and casual. If he calls her at the last minute and makes her laugh, then she may even give up one of her telephone lines. If he knocks her dead with clever ideas, projects and peculiar little pastimes, then, when she's stopped flirting with his best friend, he can command her to become his life partner. She'll probably say 'yes' and tell him that she thought he'd never get around to it. He might want to reply that it was because she always had more men around her than somebody protected by the Secret Service, but it wouldn't be a good idea.

Leo man with Cancer woman

It might seem that she wants his entire being – she does. When it comes to affairs of the heart, this woman is a conspicuous consumer. She craves his total love, attention, affection, fantasies, thoughts and dreams. In other words, she wants it all and there won't be any leftovers. She revels in romanticism. One of her frequent sexual fantasies is hearing the words 'I love you', but her favourites are 'Marry me!' If he does, he'll have a very loyal and devoted wife. If he brings her daisies and kisses her a lot, then he'll find a woman who will create a kingdom for him.

Leo man with Virgo woman

Her idea of fun is to clean the refrigerator. His is to eat what's in it. She needs extra room for her vitamins, aspirin and nasal spray. He needs to take a course just to pronounce the names of the pills she's taking. She hates dust, dirt, grime and greasy spots. Because he's not particularly fond of it either, he'll be grateful that he's found someone who will finally do something about it. She'll be forever supportive, dutiful and faithful. She finds affairs too anxiety-producing, so he doesn't need to worry if he catches her in an animated conversation in a dimly lit corner with a devastatingly handsome man – he'll be her doctor.

Leo man with Libra woman

She's always wanted a caretaker, and he's always wanted the power of looking after someone. She's submissive, smiles a lot and settles for whatever makes him happy. And because it's exactly this kind of behaviour that makes him happy, she could be the woman of his dreams. If only he was stimulated by her temperament.

Leo man with Scorpio woman

He'll wonder if she's speaking a foreign language. However, as long as she opens her mouth, he'll always be foolish enough to think he actually has a chance to understand her. But when she closes it and stares at his lower lip, forget it. All hope is lost, and so is his sanity. In her most lucid moments, this woman is an enigma, but if he's trained in palmistry, reading tea leaves or astrology, then they could be a great success. Just as long as he's not too emotionally exhausted to notice.

Needless to say the attraction here is not compelling. In terms of rapport, it would be easier for him to talk to his tortoise. Ask her what's on her mind, and after a 10-minute pause in which he'll wonder if she's gone into a trance, she'll reply 'Nothing', and that, of course, means everything.

There's no doubt about it, this woman has a lot of power. With both her eyes closed she can see right into his soul. But with both his eyes open and Superman's X-ray vision her mind still remains a mystery. If he is so bored that he's yearning for an ultimate challenge, then he's got one here. But if it's only a mystery and a thrill he's really after, then he should do himself a favour and settle for a good book.

Leo man with Sagittarius woman

He'll probably meet her in an airport, where she seems to be going in both directions. She's coming from South America and heading for Egypt for a little boat trip down the Nile, and then a night flight to the Azores. Miss Sagittarius spends more time in the air than Richard Branson.

To hold her attention he will have to become a travel

agent or a multi-millionaire with a fleet of private planes, which he'll need just to keep up with her. He'll find her conversation witty, her behaviour flighty and her mind strangely philosophical. She faces each day with a smile and a basic credo that everything is ultimately for the best. Her laughter uplifts him and her ideas inspire him. Suddenly, he'll find himself fasting, reading strange books and attending weekend yoga retreats. Like never before, he feels fantastic and full of love. Miss Sagittarius has a primitive power called vitality. It's guaranteed to capture his soul and to seduce his sensibilities – he'll never be the same.

Leo man with Capricorn woman

He'll meet her at a tennis club, but she won't be playing, she'll be standing watching and her outfit will be more smashing than his backhand. During the ski season, check the sundecks. She'll have cultivated her tan, but don't even ask to borrow her Ambre Solaire because for all she knows it's a piece of pastry. To all appearances this girl has class, but she wasn't born with it, she's paid a lot to get it. What she's seeking is her reward, and the bigger the better.

He can charm her quite easily, but if he wants to keep her he must cut out the casual flirtation. This girl is after control and in her mind nothing is casual. So when she cuts you cold, she's just being cautious. His narcissism has made her very nervous, so if he doesn't want to be abandoned he'd better behave.

Leo man with Aquarius woman

Marry her and he'll have his own private social worker, physiotherapist and recreational director. But first he has to get a chance to see her. She knows more people than a politician, and they all occupy a special place in her heart. When it comes to people, she has an inexhaustible attention span and a penchant for helping lost souls. The phone probably rings till dawn and the doorbell till at least 12.30. At 10 o'clock he'll find her lavishing warmth on the lovelorn, while at 2 am she deserts him to aid a friend.

Unlike many of his usual heart-throbs, this woman generally doesn't bother with the superficial. She has little or no interest in her appearance and usually co-ordinates her clothes as though she'd been awakened by a fire. She's different, but so genuine that even he can occasionally overlook the fact that she's wearing an embroidered work shirt to a black-tie dinner party, with a yellow badge that says 'Higher wages for banana pickers'.

Leo man with Pisces woman

She'll mope around a lot, which can get pretty boring, but what she does in bed is something else altogether. She talks through her body and what she has to say has his undivided attention. Naturally, he'll like to have her around, but because he's the restless sort it's a question of for how long. For a while they'll feed each other's dreams and the air will reek of romance. It's candlelight and love all the way. But after a certain point it can be loneliness if he starts emerging from the emotional fog unprepared.

Miss Pisces represents one of the few signs that can let the feelings flow. And while she may not be outwardly indestructible, she has strength through vulnerability. His idea of strength is the 'stiff upper lip', and so until he opens his head and heart and learns how to connect them, this woman is better off elsewhere.

Monthly and Daily Guides

JANUARY

THE SUN, AS USUAL, WILL BE coasting along in the sign of Capricorn up until the 20th. By now you probably realize that this means a lot of hard work during this period. Still, you have a consolation, your relationships with your workmates should be improving and there will be chances to have some fun and games with them.

After the 20th the Sun will be moving into your opposite sign of Aquarius. This means, my Leo friend, that you cannot expect to get your own way during the next few weeks. It is important that you listen to what other people have to say before you decide whether it is valid or not. This isn't a month for going off on your own believing that you know best. You'd be surprised what you can pick up when you have conversations with other people.

On a more personal level, Venus will be in the fiery sign of Sagittarius up until the 24th. Hopefully you're single because there'll be lots of opportunities for having fun, earning money and possibly romance. But the emphasis here is definitely on casual, so don't let that big generous heart of yours get too carried away.

Mind you, if you have a partner, they will be prone to straying. If I were you I'd make a great big fuss of them during this period if you want to save the relationship.

Mars will be entering the watery sign of Pisces on the 4th. This is not exactly the best news you've ever had because it tends to bring a certain amount of stress and strain in the life of people you are financially dependent upon, and also where official matters are concerned. You can no longer afford to tear up those brown envelopes. You may find amongst them a summons that you have ignored and that can lead you into a great deal of trouble, so do be sensible.

Financially, until the 18th anyway, you gain not only from hard work, but also perhaps from travelling, foreigners and paperwork. If you have a contract to sign, then make sure you choose a good day for doing just that.

After the 18th Mercury will be moving into your opposite sign of Aquarius. This is good news because it will bring the ability for you to make fresh starts in your intimate relationships. It will also open the lines of communication and will be bringing new people into your social life, and as a very sociable person this can only be good news.

Finally, because the planets are making a distinct pattern, it seems that you have your life well in control. But that doesn't mean you shouldn't listen to the questions and ideas of other people. You may be kicking yourself for quite some time to come if you don't. Socially, sports are well starred and matters related to children can benefit and, as I've already said, romance tends to be casual. Now look at the *Daily Guides* for further information.

Daily Guide – January

1 SATURDAY Your ruling planet, the Sun, is lining up beautifully with Saturn, so you begin a new year knowing exactly what you want, how you're going to achieve it and when. However, it might be a good idea to clear up any half-finished projects, otherwise they will only prey on your mind and distract you.

2 SUNDAY The Sun is lining up with Pluto, so you have an excellent time for making one or two minor adjustments or changes. But don't be too ambitious, major changes of direction should ideally be left until another time. This evening is well starred if you're thinking of entertaining at home, perhaps a dinner party or just a few friends.

3 MONDAY Venus is in a great aspect with Neptune. This is an especially good time then for those of you who work in a creative or artistic job. Those around are in a highly sensitive mood so no bullying please. Put a smile on your face, listen if they want to talk and then you'll be creating a lot of goodwill. Tonight is a good time for romance too.

4 TUESDAY Mars moves into the water sign of Pisces. Over the next couple of weeks, particularly on the bad days, you must stick to the letter of the law. But it's a good time for dealing with insurance matters and giving as much support to people you rely on, both at work and at home. This is not the time for stepping into centre stage however.

5 WEDNESDAY Although you like to run an organized ship you don't want to deprive anyone of their freedom of choice. The advice you offer is usually taken so it has to be good. Someone may change crucial plans on the strength of something you say. Not a time for any kind of bluffing. Only the real thing will do.

6 THURSDAY This is the day of the New Moon and it occurs in the gritty sign of Capricorn. An ideal time therefore for getting closer to people at work, for presenting your ideas and perhaps even socializing with them. On the personal side, if you want to make any kind of change this is the day for doing so. The New Moon will help you to be successful.

7 FRIDAY Your money planet, Mercury, is in touch with Pluto which seems to suggest that you're in the mood to spend money. Luckily, at this time of the year there may be some bargains on offer. If that's the case you're going to be one of the lucky ones and will find something of value. This evening, there's likely to be some news, or perhaps gossip, which will liven things up.

8 SATURDAY If you make any important decisions about the future then try not to let sentiment get in the way. Old habits die hard, and it would be the easiest thing in the world to keep things as they are. You are seen by many as a guiding light. Once you make a break with the past others will have the confidence to follow suit.

9 SUNDAY Venus is in a close aspect with Pluto, suggesting that there could be some kind of upheaval or perhaps a stumbling block for you to overcome at work. However, as a Leo, you're not going to allow a little thing like this to prevent you from making progress. But it would be a good idea not to be too ambitious as you may find yourself running on the spot, which would be very frustrating.

10 MONDAY Information picked up along the way may help you to see things differently. Impulsive stars are encouraging you to take a risk. Although you may not feel especially lucky at the moment, remember even a rank outsider can win. So pluck up your courage and use your brave streak that others envy and admire.

11 TUESDAY It is important today that you try to balance those Leo flashes of genius with a certain amount of reality. You must fight to free yourself from any kind of insecurity or phobia related to long-term prospects or finances in your professional life. The only enemy you have is yourself, so don't let your imagination work overtime.

12 WEDNESDAY Fortunately, Saturn now resumes direct movement. So any small arguments and irritations with workmates should begin to fade into oblivion. Should you be feeling at all under par, especially if you happen to have flu symptoms, then do yourself a favour and get in an early night.

13 THURSDAY Anyone who thinks you can be trampled under foot is in for a surprise. Your image may betray you as caring and generous, which no doubt you are, but you're a lot else besides that. A show of temper will fade as quickly as it flares up, but not before everyone has learned what a forceful person you really can be.

14 FRIDAY Things that are going on behind the scenes are highlighting fears and apprehension. However, you have less to worry about than most as you know how a particular set-up should be managed, even though it's falling short of expectations at the moment. Surround yourself with those who will advise you when things shift into a different gear.

15 SATURDAY You may be laying down rules and regulations you'll never enforce. Tension between loved ones means you must decide what the next stage should be. But don't be surprised if you end up giving everyone an easy way out. The stars right now can soften the hardest heart and remind you where your loyalties really lie.

16 SUNDAY Your ruling planet, the Sun, is in a beautiful aspect with Mercury. It's an ideal time for sorting out legal matters, paperwork and maybe making a fresh start in at least one direction. Those of you who are dreaming of distant shores and the sunshine, as we all tend to at this time of the year, may very well be booking a holiday.

17 MONDAY Your ruling planet, the Sun, lines up with Jupiter in a rather adverse way. You need to watch out because your judgement is completely off. It's possible that you're being far too ambitious or optimistic about a relationship or some other matter. If this should be the case then lower your sights and you will save yourself a lot of trouble.

18 TUESDAY Mars is in an explosive aspect with Pluto. This suggests that there could be a certain amount of tension, stress or argument in connection with the family, or perhaps property matters. If you're in the throes of buying a new home then let matters wait for another 24 hours before going ahead.

19 WEDNESDAY Mercury moves into your opposite sign of Aquarius. Therefore over the next few weeks or so it's likely that you will be meeting many new and stimulating people. If you're already in a relationship, it could be taking off in a different direction, much to your surprise, but whatever happens should be to your advantage so don't worry.

20 THURSDAY The Sun moves into the airy sign of Aquarius. This is certainly good news for those of you who are in the teaching profession or in work related to foreign countries. You know exactly what you are doing and you won't hesitate to say so if others try to put you down over the next few weeks. Keep faith with yourself.

21 FRIDAY Today is the day of the Full Moon and unfortunately it happens to fall in your sign. You may wake up in a grumpy frame of mind and take out your frustrations and irritations on other people throughout the day as well as the evening. This, of course, is destructive and will cause bad feeling, so use this time for putting the finishing touches to work that has been hanging around and avoid at all cost doing anything new.

22 SATURDAY The Sun today continues in your opposite sign of Aquarius. Over the next few weeks or so it may be necessary for you to cooperate with other people more than is usual, both at home and at work. There's a chance, too, that romance will receive a boost because of this. So if you're single, keep your eyes open because you never know.

23 SUNDAY There may have been some sort of intrigue going on but you're in a position to force everything out into the open as far as work or health matters are concerned right now. Don't be hard on those who have been feeding rumours and fanning flames of unrest. Without them you would never have been forced to lead instead of follow, and you wouldn't have learned all you know now. Make use of every bit of information received and create something remarkable for the future.

24 MONDAY It might be a good idea to give up on a wild scheme if you must, but don't let your inventiveness be used against you. If there were more like you around, certain people wouldn't suffer the way they do. You have at least tried, even though you may have lost out in the end. You are way ahead of those who just simply sat still.

25 TUESDAY Mercury will be moving into your opposite sign of Aquarius, throwing a rosy glow over all of your close relationships, both at work and at home. Now, if you are totally unattached then you have a couple of weeks when you could meet somebody who will lighten up your life in a big way. Those already in a relationship may even be thinking of naming the day.

26 WEDNESDAY There's no point in taking a tough line if you're likely to capitulate in the end. True, things have gone far enough and a fragile set-up will break down unless guidelines are observed or a code of practice followed. The stars are illuminating qualities that set you apart from the rest. Why not use them?

27 THURSDAY A cash crisis must be averted if all your hard work is to pay off. Although you may know what steps need to be taken, you mustn't charge ahead and do just what you like. Take into account the feelings of those who have shared your load. They might have very different views from your own.

28 FRIDAY Venus is lining up with Neptune. This is an excellent time for creative work and also a time when you must go out of your way to co-operate with other people. This evening you're at your most attractive, and so if you are single, spruce yourself up and get into the limelight.

29 SATURDAY Your patience is wearing thin and close companions may bear the brunt of it today. Mischievous stars are in operation so you'll be in no mood for indifference or apathy. A tough line of questioning could lead to a slanging match, but at least you'll learn all you need to know about other people's motives and intentions.

30 SUNDAY Do put your efforts into a project that shows signs of dying on its feet. Only an injection of your own brand of energy and imagination can save it. It would be a pity to see something fail when it has such a following. Just don't think you can do everything yourself; you can't and nor should you. Get help.

31 MONDAY Your ruling planet, the Sun, lines up with sensible, practical Saturn. You couldn't have a better aspect therefore for making important decisions and moves. Furthermore, if you have been covered in confusion where a particular personal problem is concerned, this is a time for unravelling it as well as your good self. Concentration is excellent if you're working on anything intricate.

FEBRUARY

DURING THIS MONTH the majority of the planets seem to be above the horizon. This seems to suggest there will be a tendency for you to be drawn to that which is novel. On the negative side you could start many relationships and many jobs but be uninterested in finishing them. This won't do your reputation any good, Leo, so make sure that you don't leave things half done because people at work, and perhaps your family, will begin to lose faith in you.

Mars will be entering Aries on the 12th and regardless of your own sex it seems that your male friends are influencing you more than usual. Perhaps they are handing on some useful advice, or just simply helping you out of a difficult situation, either way can't be bad.

The placing of Venus means that work will be pleasant and you may even find romance in connection with it, but don't take it too seriously. While that of Mercury suggests news coming from a foreign country, perhaps an offer of some description or maybe it's simply a case that you're booking your summer holiday. All in all, February doesn't seem to have a great deal against it. Now look at the *Daily Guides* for further information.

1 TUESDAY Someone is hoping you will give a sparkling performance of what you do best. But you won't want to be involved in what you know could be an embarrassing experience. All sorts of incentives are being used in an effort to win you around. Don't waver. The carrot can be as bad as the stick.

2 WEDNESDAY Your ruler, the Sun, is lining up with Pluto, making this an ideal day for carrying out any kind of change that your heart desires. Mind you, if you're unlucky, there may be a stumbling block in your way. But instead of ranting and raving, see if you can quietly manoeuvre your way around it, it shouldn't be that difficult.

3 THURSDAY Venus is in a beautiful aspect with Saturn, suggesting that much can be achieved at work, particularly if you are working in a team or in anything creative. If you need any kind of advice, then it is time to turn to somebody far more experienced than your good self.

4 FRIDAY There could be moments of real surprise as a little light dawns on hidden areas of your life. Emotionally, you could do with more affectionate support, but maybe what you lack is the willingness to give first. Remember that what goes around, comes around, so go where the whim takes you. Friends could be a little unpredictable but to balance this there may be good financial news if you look in the right place. Your persuasive powers are clearly working.

5 SATURDAY Today is the day of the New Moon and it falls in your opposite sign of Aquarius, which can be good news depending on circumstances. You may meet new and exciting people and a fresh romance could get off the ground. Certainly this is a time for listening to what other people have to say, because their advice will be sound.

6 SUNDAY The Sun is in a beautiful aspect with Uranus, and so this day should be filled with harmony, peace and perhaps a certain amount of romance. You're in accord with other people in all areas of life and will be feeling very contented and smug by the time this day is through. Much good work can be done.

7 MONDAY Your money planet, Mercury, is lining up with Neptune. There may be then some kind of financial muddle or perhaps you may buy something that really isn't up to standard. So don't make major purchases during this time. Wait until a better one otherwise you will have reason to regret your action.

8 TUESDAY Even though close partners are on hand with more support, you are still giving marginally more than you are getting in return. However, one reward may come through almost instantly, so try hard to look grateful. Financially, you are on your toes, so nothing will escape your eagle eye. An impulse buy will do you the world of good and make it easier to be generous to a companion in a flamboyant way.

9 WEDNESDAY No one can deny that you are in

pretty good form. Close partnerships have their ups and downs, but when they do work they work exceptionally well. You'll definitely have that mischievous twinkle in your eye, which means you will want to spread your social favours around very generously. No one among your wide circle of friends will miss out as you positively seduce them into laughing more openly.

10 THURSDAY No one crowds you into a corner when you want to fly away. You have an electric energy which fizzles, sparkles and pops when you feel that you need some more elbow room. Companions, at arms length, will find you stimulating. Only those close by may discover you've quite a high voltage if they try to send you off down a path not of your choosing. Paying attention to your diet and exercise regime will pay off.

11 FRIDAY With your sweetest smile at the ready, you are charming all the right people at work or out socializing. You may have an ulterior motive, but others will never notice. Just make sure you are giving yourself a chance to relax as well. The planets are hinting at a way of unshackling one restraining situation. The family may need a little gentle pressure to change direction, but given time you can be pretty sure that they will do as you wish.

12 SATURDAY Mars will be moving into the fire sign of Aries, beginning a period when those you are financially dependent on may be stressed and argumentative. See what you can do to give them some backing and try to entice them out so that they can really relax. The old hormones are jumping around this evening, so literally anything can happen and probably will.

13 SUNDAY Mercury is in a difficult aspect with Pluto, and because of this you may suffer from mental blocks from time to time, especially at work. The best thing to do is to turn your attention to matters that you can literally do with your eyes closed and leave more challenging tasks until another day. Be sure that you stay out of arguments with loved ones this evening. They may be trying to deliberately bait you for reasons best known to themselves.

14 MONDAY Out on the social scene you look assured, almost sophisticated. Only those who know intimately can see the ebbs and flows of your moods. Just as you decide to move way, you suddenly switch on to the opposite tack. Concentrate at home on creating the most tasteful and elegant atmosphere. You need a calm nest, preferably one filled with relaxing music, good movies on the video and plenty of treats.

15 TUESDAY Today is the day when Jupiter changes sign and moves into the earthy sign of Taurus. For the remainder of the year then Lady Luck will be on your side where professional matters are concerned, and some of you may be receiving some kind of reward or even promotion. There will be times when colleagues will be envious or simply pleasantly surprised. But whatever occurs it's going to be all to the good.

16 WEDNESDAY A tough routine at work means you could feel life is getting a touch unbalanced, so embrace any chance to let your hair down. Be mildly outrageous, if that feels good, with loved ones or friends. They can be rebellious when it suits them, so you might as well have your moment of freedom as well. Slow down long enough for one in-depth conversation. You will emerge enriched with a gem of wisdom.

17 THURSDAY Unconventional friends will keep you on your toes or sitting on the edge of your seat. You can never quite decide whether they are being serious or not when they get into an outrageous mood. Pick and choose what you want to do and with whom. There are choices for you to make and plenty of variety. You can smartly slide out of corners and flit from flower to flower. Yet you must try and find some quality time for yourself as well.

18 FRIDAY Venus will be moving into your opposite sign of Aquarius. Over the next couple of weeks or so there's going to be a great deal of peace and harmony where all relationships are concerned. However, if you happen to be at a loose end then keep a high profile when socializing because somebody who is really worthwhile could be about to enter your scene.

19 SATURDAY Today is the day of the Full Moon and

unfortunately it falls in the cash area of your chart. Hang on to your possessions otherwise you may lose something precious. Avoid the shops because your extravagant taste could make a great big hole in your bank account, which will be something you will live to regret for some time to come. At least Full Moons allow you a time for putting finishing touches to all kinds of situations as well as work.

20 SUNDAY Today is a day when your ruling planet, the Sun, moves into Pisces. You will temporarily take on some of the characteristics of this sign, becoming more gentle, romantic and maybe even indecisive. The last of these is no bad thing because at times you can be too sure of yourself and can fail to cover all contingencies, but not now.

21 MONDAY Your money planet, Mercury, moves into retrograde action. Until this situation rights itself you may feel as if you're marching on the spot where cash matters are concerned. On no account should you sign important paperwork because it could be a source of loss. Travelling may be complicated, particularly methods of transport, such as your car.

22 TUESDAY Venus is in a beautiful aspect with Neptune. Therefore, this is an ideal day for those of you who work at all creatively. You'll have ideas that will rock other people on their heels and will make a big impression. This evening is a fine time for romance, so if you are single make sure you are looking good and get out into the big wide world.

23 WEDNESDAY A generous present will be more than enough to lift the tension at home. Now you know you can move ahead more freely emotionally, it means you have a good many more options financially and in every other way. Negotiate with intimate partners, since you need to know you share similar values. You'll be overexcitable at one point, but will move happily into a delicious, indulgent and confident mood.

24 THURSDAY You're finding more and more good excuses to try out new approaches to almost everything in your life. The old strait-laced, or at least square side of your character, who never budged from habits and patterns set a long time ago, has now disappeared. You are positively experimental, socially, romantically, financially and at work. A breath of fresh air blowing through your routine keeps you feeling alive and vibrant.

25 FRIDAY Life behind the scenes may be heavy going, but on the surface you are skipping around like a spring lamb. But just don't scratch the surface too hard. You might as well socialize with people who make you feel charmed and charming. Your efforts to shake yourself away from the past will work in the long term, but don't be too impatient. There have to be pauses along the way for you to play and relax.

26 SATURDAY Acting as a peace-maker, you can soothe, smooth and cheer as you go. Although at times you wish someone would do the same for you. Do stand up for your rights as well as pushing for other people's comforts. It may take a little lateral strategy to work out how you manage both, but you are the most versatile thinker around at this time. Accept every invitation that comes your way. You will sparkle to good effect and probably overspend, but won't care.

27 SUNDAY In spite of promises made you have always been afraid you'll be let down over a work or financial issue. You are handling something complex and the stars suggest you should at last see signs that now others really are behind you. Provided you know what you want in the end you'll have no trouble in getting it.

28 MONDAY Venus is lining up with Pluto and because of this there are likely to be changes at work, or perhaps where family and property matters are concerned. Should you be single then literally anything can happen and probably will, providing of course that you are prepared to get out and about.

29 TUESDAY Mars is in an explosive aspect with Pluto, which could create a certain amount of tension, argument and bad feeling at home, or perhaps in connection with property. Someone has to see common sense and act more fairly and, quite frankly Leo, it might just as well be you. So see what you can do, otherwise the month will end on a low note and that would be a pity.

MARCH

DURING THIS MONTH there is a distinct possibility of you starting relationships, jobs and projects which you will not follow through. This may lead other people to doubt your integrity. However, with the Sun, Venus and Mercury in Pisces it seems that you're more than usually concerned about people you are financially dependent upon, whether your boss or partner. You may be considering beginning a professional relationship or partnership, and if so this should be successful.

Fortunately, Mercury is in direct movement from the 14th and so if you need to travel or put your signature to important paperwork, you have an ideal time for doing just that. Those of you with friends in a foreign country are likely to be hearing from them very soon.

Mars will be coasting along in the fire sign of Aries, therefore you must take care not to overwork that busy brain. There's a strong chance that you'll take on too much and only realize it at a far later date. Remember that haste often leads to inefficiency and that's something that you really cannot bear to be accused of, but it may just happen at this time. If you're involved in a legal matter then take professional advice. You may think you know best but I'm afraid this just isn't true.

Jupiter and Saturn at the zenith at your chart means that any hard work or extra responsibility you take on is sure to bring in rewards in the future. So don't think twice about doing so, you'll be glad that you did.

With all of the planets situated at the top of your chart there is a distinct possibility, as already mentioned, that you may start things but will lose interest quickly.

Although this not usually your way, even you can step out of character and you seem to be doing so in a certain amount of style at this time. Now look at the *Daily Guides* for further information.

1 WEDNESDAY You're good at forming useful associations. Someone is keen to help you out with a project that's already taken up too much of your time. You're in danger of clutching at straws, however. Go over the details once more and make sure you're not reading more into a suggestion than actually exists.

2 THURSDAY Today could be a confusing time because the stars are extremely busy, so one minute you're up, the next minute you're down. During the morning, workmates and loved ones may be helpful. But during the afternoon and evening, they may be deliberately aggravating and out of sorts. The best thing you can do is to get yourself into an adaptable frame of mind and don't take anyone or anything too seriously for the time being.

3 FRIDAY Some family affairs are moving into a different league. The stars suggest others will be slightly dazed and confused, and will need time to think. You, on the other hand, are in the mood for instant decisions and impulse buys. Doing what you want in your own way and in your good time is a great tonic.

4 SATURDAY You have talent and resources, but you're unsure of what to do next. There's no point in making a move until you know exactly where you should be heading. Try seeking guidance. It sometimes takes another pair of eyes to see something that's been in front of your nose all along.

5 SUNDAY No matter how sound somebody else's idea is you seem to think an even better one is about to be produced. Make no final commitments until you have exhausted all other possibilities. The minute you give the green light to plans you're not entirely sure of there will be regrets and recriminations in the future.

6 MONDAY Today is the day of the New Moon and it falls in the watery sign of Pisces. There could therefore be a brand new cycle starting in the life of somebody you're financially dependent upon, whether a partner or boss, but either way you're going to gain indirectly. As always with New Moons it is a great time for trying something new, whether it's a new look or perhaps a hobby.

7 TUESDAY A loved one may be tired of playing guessing games. So why not give a full explanation of your movements and actions? It's a sure way to scotch any rumours concerning your behaviour. You have decisions to make and actions to take. It's time to cut through all the gossip, petty politics and foolish pranks.

8 WEDNESDAY There has been a lot of talk about travel projects or new ideas that offer something for everybody. However, someone is threatening to veto plans purely out of a desire to spoil the fun. You have limited power until you prove how many people you have on your side.

9 THURSDAY Your ruling planet, the Sun, is lining up with Mars. This will be increasing your energy, your enthusiasm and your zest for living. Furthermore, those hormones of yours will begin jumping and hopefully they will wait until you get out this evening, because it wouldn't be a good idea to become temporarily involved with anyone connected with work.

10 FRIDAY There seems to be a great deal of emphasis on cash matters on this particular day. You may have a financial decision to make but this is far from the ideal time for doing so. Instead, turn your attention into other directions and in the meantime make sure you don't overspend.

11 SATURDAY Because you have done so much for others, they forget you might welcome some backing on occasions, and that's exactly what you'll be hoping for fairly soon. It's important to adopt the right frame of mind. Don't be too proud to ask for help from people who know what the next stage of the situation should entail.

12 SUNDAY You are inclined to be impatient and short-tempered when you are dealing with intensely personal problems. Avoid a tendency to use material issues as a weapon. Remain open-minded in your approach, otherwise you could well become involved in unnecessary conflict.

13 MONDAY Venus will be moving into the watery sign of Pisces. This will be throwing a rosy glow over the affairs of people you are financially dependent upon. You'll also find it a good deal easier to talk to loved ones, and so if you have any grievances get them out into the open. Remember to do so with a certain amount of love and caring rather than brute force.

14 TUESDAY Luckily Mercury, your money planet, has decided to resume direct movement and so the chaos of recent weeks will slowly begin to evaporate. From hereon in travel matters are well starred and you can attend to paperwork in the confidence that you will be doing exactly the right thing.

15 WEDNESDAY Pluto will be going into retrograde movement, which means that you begin a period where property and home matters could be complicated and difficult. Try not to be too critical and overbearing with loved ones, because where they may normally keep quiet there could be a gigantic explosion which will cause bad feelings all round.

16 THURSDAY Not everyone has your instinct for what's right and what's wrong. The stars should make you determined to help others get their just desserts. No one expects you to stick your neck out, but if you don't your conscience may get the better of you. However, if you do, there'll be plenty of reason for celebration.

17 FRIDAY Although you like to run a tight ship you don't want to deprive anyone of their freedom of choice. The advice you offer is usually taken so it has to be good. Someone may change crucial plans on the strength of something you say. This is no time for bluffing. Only the real thing will do.

18 SATURDAY Venus is in a beautiful aspect with Jupiter, and therefore at work there will be a happy atmosphere and plenty of cooperation. So much so that you'll be full of energy this evening and ready to enjoy yourself. Make sure you get out and about because this is also a good evening for romance.

19 SUNDAY The Sun will be moving into the fire sign of Aries. This is the area of your chart devoted to people that you are financially dependent upon. Such people will be much more confident about their future and their current good mood over the next few days or so is likely to rub off on you in a positive way.

20 MONDAY Today is the day of the Full Moon and it occurs in the earthy sign of Virgo. This is the financial area of your chart, so for some unlucky few there may be a loss of income or perhaps a loss of a precious possession. In any event, all Lions should think twice before making important moves on this day.

21 TUESDAY Even if you have big ideas and foolproof plans things can go wrong, especially if someone is working against you. You must have now realized it's not enough just to investigate problems and difficulties. You must also discover their source, so that appropriate action can be taken to see that it doesn't happen again.

22 WEDNESDAY You seem to feel you have been in one place for too long. Do something about your itchy feet because others tire of your restlessness and everyone's patience wears thin. Surprise developments may offer you just what you've been waiting for, but you will have to say yes very quickly.

23 THURSDAY Mars will be moving to the zenith point of your chart into the sign of Taurus. It looks then as if you're about to start a hard-working period. Keep your head down and tackle what needs to be done. This could eventually lead to some sort of gain and maybe promotion for some of you.

24 FRIDAY If you're making any important decisions about the future try not to let sentiment get in the way. Old habits die hard and it would be the easiest thing in the world to keep things as they are. You are seen by many as a guiding light. Once you make a break with the past others will have the confidence to follow suit.

Daily Guide – March

25 SATURDAY Mercury is lining up in a beautiful aspect with Jupiter, and so this is a day when you can take a calculated risk with your hard-earned cash. But this doesn't mean backing some three-legged horse, otherwise you'll be regretting it for quite some time to come, so do be sensible. A document signed on this day will be profitable.

26 SUNDAY Your ruling planet, the Sun, is in a beautiful aspect with Neptune. This softens your personality as well as your heart. The only problem is that there is a suggestion here that you'll fall easy prey to a sob story. But use your logic and your common sense and you'll be able to distinguish the truth from fabrication.

27 MONDAY Information picked up along the way may help you to see things differently. Impulsive stars are encouraging you to take a risk. Remember even rank outsiders can triumph, so, just for the moment, pluck up your courage. Others may envy and admire you for it.

28 TUESDAY Anyone who thinks you can be trampled over is in for a surprise. You're more than just a sensitive and caring person. An outburst of temper will fade as quickly as it flares up, but not before everyone has learned what a forceful individual you can be.

29 WEDNESDAY Give up on a wild schme if you must, but don't let your sense of adventure be used against you. If there were more like you around certain individuals wouldn't suffer the way they do. You have at least tried, even though you may have lost out in the end. That's better than never even bothering.

30 THURSDAY Your money planet, Mercury, is badly aspected by Pluto. Hang on to your possessions and when out shopping stick only to essentials. If you imagine that you can pick up a bargain at this time, I'm afraid you're in for a nasty shock and so is your bank manager.

31 FRIDAY Mars is in a difficult aspect with Pluto, so travelling from place to place could be complicated as well as chaotic. Curb any kind of impulsive move or important decision, it simply isn't the time to put anything at risk. You'll lose out if you do.

APRIL

APRIL IS A MONTH when you'll be seriously attempting some sort of self-improvement. It may be that you'll sign up for a course, or some of you may be booking your holiday and this is cause for a certain amount of excitement. On a more personal level, when it comes to romance, especially if you're single, you'll be drawn to those who have strange accents and who come from different shores and cultures. This may initially fascinate you but as usual once you have decided that you have found out all about them you'll be preparing to move on.

If you're involved in any kind of legal matter this month, you are sure to do very well. Furthermore, many of you will be planning a trip, possibly for business or pleasure, in the very near future and money spent on this will not be wasted. Workwise, try not to overdo it. There's a tendency for you to go to extremes and you may finish up on the sick list, which is no place for any red-blooded Lion to be. There's nothing you hate more than sitting in bed alone. You'll fidget, toss and turn and make yourself feel worse. You need a sensible friend or a relative to keep you under control. Now look at the *Daily Guides* for further information.

1 SATURDAY Your ruling planet, the Sun, is lining up with Pluto and so you begin this month with a strong desire to clear the decks and start again. There may be a project or a hobby that has been hanging around because you have lost enthusiasm and perhaps you're kidding yourself you'll pick it up at a later date. Face facts, and then you'll know what you should keep and what should be disposed of.

2 SUNDAY There's no point in taking a tough line if you're likely to capitulate in the end. True, things have gone far enough and a fragile set-up will break down unless guidelines are observed and a code of practice followed. The stars are illuminating qualities that set you apart from the rest. Why not use them?

3 MONDAY A financial crisis must be averted if all your hard work is to pay off. Although you may know what steps should be taken next, you mustn't charge ahead and do just what you think. Take into account the feelings of those who have shared the load. They might have very different views from your own.

4 TUESDAY Today is the day of the New Moon and it falls in the fiery sign of Aries. If you have a loved one in another country then you're likely to be hearing from them. If you have recently taken any kind of test or examination, then the results should be on their way and it should be good news. As always with New Moons, you can begin anything new and that includes relationships.

5 WEDNESDAY This is a day for reflection and one when you need to understand that you should try to react to situations and problems in a more constructive fashion. Try putting your principles first, rather than your popularity with other people. You will soon learn how to deal with long-standing financial or material problems.

6 THURSDAY Mars is in a beautiful aspect with Jupiter and this provides you with an extremely lively and interesting day. Accept invitations for events in the future which could be quite exciting. If you're out this evening and are single, you could meet someone special, but I'm afraid it is only a physical attraction. Or maybe that won't matter.

7 FRIDAY Venus moves into the fiery sign of Aries. This is the part of your chart devoted to long-distance travelling and higher education. If you're taking any kind of test, then the stars will be on your side. If you're booking a holiday for the very near future, you're sure to be getting a bargain and will be feeling very pleased with yourself. Furthermore, from now on you may be attracted to those who come from foreign lands.

8 SATURDAY Put your efforts into a project that shows signs of dying on its feet. Only an injection of your own brand of energy and inspiration can save it. It would be a pity to see something fail when it has such a following. However, don't think you can do everything yourself. You can't, so get help.

9 SUNDAY Someone is hoping you will give a sparkling performance of what you do best. But you won't want to be involved in what you know could be an embarrassing experience. All sorts of incentives are being used in an attempt to win you round, but don't waver.

10 MONDAY Your ruling planet, the Sun, is lining up with Uranus, giving you a certain amount of magnetism and an attraction that others cannot miss. If you are single, there could be a meeting of hearts this evening, so make sure you keep a high profile and get out and about. If you already have a loved one, then you're in for a romantic evening.

11 TUESDAY Venus is lining up with Neptune, and so at work you must not take anything for granted.

Certainly, give full rein to your creativity but make sure that you have finished all those tedious jobs that you would so much prefer to ignore. Fail to do so and I'm afraid you could be letting yourself in for a good deal of trouble.

12 WEDNESDAY Travel plans that once seemed doomed should show signs of improvement. Your expectations must be realistic, however. Having pushed your way to the front of the queue, you need to take a more realistic approach. Be diplomatic and you will soon be on your way.

13 THURSDAY Mercury is moving into the fiery sign of Aries, which is certainly going to be helpful for those of you who are either travelling or are involved in litigation of any description. There's a possibility, too, that money can be gained by listening to the ideas of a person who comes from a different background from yourself. This is definitely a day for being as open-minded as possible, so don't turn anything down until you've had time to think about it.

14 FRIDAY Mars is in aspect with Saturn and so the pace of this day will be uneven. One minute you're given the go ahead and as soon as you do you seem to run into a brick wall. Be respectful of people older than yourself. They may be trying to give you good advice, but you're in one of those moods when you simply don't want to know. But then a Lion always prefers to keep to the helm of their own life, even if it goes in the wrong direction.

15 SATURDAY No one doubts that you deserve a break. But those in a position to acknowledge your achievements have their hands tied with red tape. Patience will serve you a great deal better than impulsive actions or a sudden change of direction. Whatever you achieve in the end will be worth waiting for.

16 SUNDAY Venus is in a beautiful aspect with Pluto. Although there may be changes in connection with your job they are going to be beneficial in the future, even if right now you cannot see exactly how. Get out this evening. There's a possibility of you making interesting contacts as well as new friends. Romance looks slightly unlikely, unless of course you already have a partner.

17 MONDAY If you feel you are stuck in a rut, you have nobody but yourself to blame. Meanwhile, the planets will provide a chance to strike a deal that you turned your back on first time around. Take a risk and you'll open doors most people aren't even aware of, but do nothing and the opportunity will disappear.

18 TUESDAY Today is the day of the Full Moon and it occurs in the air sign of Libra. There's a warning here not to be too impulsive, especially where intricate work is concerned because mistakes can occur. Check out methods of transports, particularly on short trips, a bicycle or motorbike may very well let you down. Well, when there's a Full Moon anything can happen so take preventive action and leave nothing to chance.

19 WEDNESDAY Does it feel like you're getting nowhere fast? Do money or family concerns seem never ending? Although you're not aware of it, a chain of events has been set in motion and no amount of disruption can halt its progress. A breakthrough is imminent. All you have to do is wait and have faith in your abilities.

20 THURSDAY The Sun will be moving into the gritty sign of Taurus, which is the work and status part of your chart. From hereon in you will be focusing intensely on work matters, determined to get ahead and perhaps neglecting other sides of life. Should this be the case, then I'm afraid there are going to be some loud complaints from loved ones, so learn how to distribute your energies more fairly.

21 FRIDAY Your money planet, Mercury, lines up with Pluto. Therefore for the lucky few there may be a fresh beginning where money is concerned, possibly a small win or a chance to begin a new job. This evening, there seems to be a great deal of activity, either you're entertaining or people are turning up completely out of the blue. Whichever applies, it'll be an enjoyable time.

22 SATURDAY Break the habit of taking work worries home with you. Far better to put them to the back of your mind then return refreshed and inspired. A clash between the planets may force you to implement changes that some will oppose. Your instincts for who can and who can't be trusted will save the day.

23 SUNDAY Venus is in a beautiful aspect with Uranus and so just for once people who are closest to you, at work and at home, are in a good mood and ready to listen to your gripes and your groans. Remember, too, that they have feelings and they are at their most sensitive, so be loving when you've had your chance to grumble.

24 MONDAY You may stumble across a problem that could raise a number of financial, social or personal issues. Tact and diplomacy are required if you are to avoid a dramatic scene of some kind and you must not take things any further until you are sure of the facts. If you jump to conclusions, you'll lose out in the end.

25 TUESDAY You may be tempted to join forces with someone you barely know, but it would be wise to stop and think again. A complex pattern involving the stars indicates the sort of situation you would rather do without. Anyway, your life is dramatic enough without involving yourself in somebody else's financial troubles. Try flying solo. No one can promise everything will go the way you want, but the really important things will.

26 WEDNESDAY Your ruling planet, the Sun, lines up with Neptune. This is all to the good if you are creative because you'll have inspiration pouring out of your ears. If, however, your job entails a great deal of intricate detail, then you will need to double-check everything several times, because with this planetary set-up mistakes are so easily made and overlooked.

27 THURSDAY After going around in circles for so long you just want to get somewhere soon. But why place so much emphasis on finding answers when you're not sure what the questions should be? Put your faith in those you trust unconditionally. Believe what you hear.

28 FRIDAY A battle is raging and you're in a position to steer things to their conclusion. A loved one is harbouring a grudge that could affect your work or home life. Clear the air, then decide what should be done next. Your views will be respected above and beyond anyone else's. Act now.

29 SATURDAY You may have spoken endlessly about a new scheme, but now you want to be seen doing something instead of just talking about it. However, with the planetary set-up it would be better to let things hang fire for a few more days. Others will be pleased you delayed proceedings until you are much more sure of your ground.

30 SUNDAY Don't ignore the voice of reason even if you don't think your freedom is in jeopardy. If you make high-powered moves before the time is right, you will create a bad impression in the eyes of those who count. Be practical and wait for the green light. Work or finances may improve beyond all recognition.

MAY

THIS IS PROBABLY ONE OF the most ambitious parts of the year for you. Not only is the Sun at the zenith of your chart, so that you are concentrating on being a success, it is accompanied by Mercury, Jupiter, Saturn and Venus. This conglomeration of planets can result in either confusion or a hectic and fulfilling life. When it comes to romance, it's most likely to occur indirectly through your job or through people you meet while going about your everyday business. But don't expect to meet anyone who is going to be of any great importance. Enjoy the fling if that's what it is and then be on your way.

Those of you who are considering beginning a new line of study, or perhaps a professional partnership, will have chosen an ideal time for doing so. Don't be surprised if you bump into an above average number of people born under the sign of the Bull. When this occurs prick those ears up and listen to the advice you are being given, because you can be sure that it is sound.

Mars' placing in Gemini from the 4th onwards will certainly be gingering up your social life. It is your male friends who will be the most important right now. Team sports will do well, too, but you need to be on your guard against strains and sprains, so don't be too enthusiastic and watch your step.

May seems to be a thoroughly enjoyable time, mainly because you haven't got time to draw breath and that's exactly what you like. When a Leo has time on his/her hands then boredom, resentment and bad-temper tend to set in. But I don't think that's going to occur during this month. Now look at the *Daily Guides* for further information.

1 MONDAY You're keen to nurture a special relationship or create something unique. But try to accept that there are some things that cannot be made to work overnight. Time and patience must be devoted to this project. What's the hurry anyway? You'll do fine, so proceed at a steady pace and not at a breakneck speed.

2 TUESDAY The Moon is in touch with Pluto and although things are moving fast they may not always be moving in the direction you would like. However, this particular day could make you consider giving up all hope of getting your own way in the end. Remember, however, that loved ones know what you want to achieve and you'll never lack support. This time next week you'll find things look quite different.

3 WEDNESDAY Today that fiery planet, Mars, will be moving into Gemini. This is the friendship and acquaintanceship part of your life, which is likely to be energized. However, it may not be positive unless you are careful, because certain people will be impatient and won't take any shilly-shallying from you, which in turn could offend. It may be hard for you to get through this next few weeks without falling out with at least someone, so do try to turn on that charm.

4 THURSDAY Today the New Moon falls at the zenith of your chart. You couldn't have a better aspect for making changes where work matters are concerned. Do keep a high profile and don't be afraid to let other people know what you are thinking. They are likely to be impressed and this, of course, will provide you with a boost to that sensitive ego.

5 FRIDAY Mars has now moved into the air sign of Gemini and because of this, regardless of your own sex, it seems to be the male friends who will be important over the coming weeks. Now you know where to go if you need any advice or help. However, also remember that from time to time you may become a little impatient, but if you give in to this you may ruin an old friendship and that would be a great pity.

6 SATURDAY Your money planet, Mercury, is lining up with Pluto, which could dig a big hole in your finances. Stick to your daily expenses and forget about major purchases for the time being. At least until you have a had a chance to check your bank account, otherwise you'll be making a big mistake.

7 SUNDAY Your ruling planet, the Sun, is lining up with lucky Jupiter, and so you're in high spirits which will attract other people. You may even take one or two calculated risks, and as long as you don't go completely over the top they should pay off. A wonderful day for trying to find romance, too, as others simply can't resist you.

8 MONDAY After the wonderful day of yesterday, today you're faced with the unfortunate fact that Uranus is preparing for retrograde action. This means that from now on those closest to you, both at work and at home, are unlikely to be cooperative and there will be times when you will be feeling somewhat isolated. Luckily, you are a self-sufficient person, so no doubt you'll bite your lip, hide that soft heart and simply get on with things.

9 TUESDAY Neptune's suggests that there could be a certain amount of confusion in the lives of people who you are financially dependent upon. See what you can do to offer some encouragement, or perhaps just a large dollop of love. You can be quite sure that either or both will be most welcome.

10 WEDNESDAY The Sun is in a difficult aspect with Uranus and so you'll need to tread very carefully to avoid a rift appearing in a relationship. Mind you, if you want to finish a relationship that has been hanging on for far too long and one in which you've lost all interest, well this is the time for doing so, but make sure you act with kindness and abruptness.

11 THURSDAY Just as you've decided to get a grip on finances, muddle seems to be descending. However, it's only temporary, so just shelve plans for today and relax. Not all the advice coming your way is sound, so if you must make a decision, be sure to read the fine print and be suspicious instead of skipping blithely ahead. The stars hint at a need for peace, so retreat when possible into familiar surroundings.

12 FRIDAY Mars is in a friendly aspect with Neptune today. Therefore, people you are financially dependent upon, whether your partner or your boss, will be in high spirits. If you have any good creative ideas that you want to present to them, you're provided with the ideal day for doing just that. Get out this evening, too, because you've plenty of energy left over and want to have fun.

13 SATURDAY Messiness is not usually typical of a sign like yours. You like to make sure that everything is in place. You are not a perfectionist like Virgo, but even so you can still be sharp when it comes to lack of organization or untidy workmates. However, it might be sensible to rise graciously above other people's inadequacies since you know you have shortcomings yourself. Keep an eye on cash.

14 SUNDAY Your money planet, Mercury, now moves into the sign of Gemini. This suggests that friends and acquaintances will find it relatively easy to part you from your money. It's not that they're trying to con you, but it may be that their tastes for entertainment or fun are very expensive and as a Leo you hate to lose face. You need to make a choice, either come clean or pay the price at a later date, which could be quite considerable.

15 MONDAY Trying to pin down a jelly is not easy; nor is getting one close partner to come clean. They seem to relax when you insist on hard facts. Be sensitive to the atmosphere. You are a fire sign with a healthy sixth sense so you can generally guess what is coming. Reading between the lines may produce more answers than straight questions. Just be kind, sensitive and patient and all will be revealed eventually.

16 TUESDAY It is understandable that you want to put your life on a more steady basis. However, you seem to be using a bulldozer to open a door. What you must first do is to try to relax and not be quite so tough on yourself. You can be sure that loved ones, friends and relatives will like you for what you are and not for what use you can be to them.

17 WEDNESDAY Being a minor hypochondriac, you always like to know what the latest health fads are, especially right now because you are keen to try new approaches. Luckily, you have common sense as well as curiosity, so are unlikely to end up with some dubious concoction. You do have higher levels of nervous tension and sensitivity than most, so you need to find ways of soothing and pampering yourself from time to time.

18 THURSDAY Today is the day of the Full Moon and it occurs in the water sign of Scorpio. This is the area of your chart devoted to family and property matters where complications could occur. However, if you're waiting for news in connection with a new home, then this might just be the day when you're asked to sign on the dotted line. If so, put it off for a couple days; I'm sure you can come up with some excuse.

19 FRIDAY Venus is in a beautiful aspect with Saturn. Although work may be hard and you may be given extra responsibility, the rewards in the future will be worthwhile, so push ahead and be cheerful. If you want advice on your love life, go to a more experienced friend this evening.

20 SATURDAY Your weak point is often too strong a sense of other people's suffering. Soaking in their pain or distress can slow you down. Just at the moment you need to be pushing ahead and getting your act together. If you can stop sacrificing yourself for everyone else and look to see what you need, which may at first seem selfish, then oddly enough, in the long term, you will do more good. You will build a solid platform from which to operate.

21 SUNDAY The Sun will be moving into Gemini and for you that is the friendship and acquaintanceship area of life. You're in for a good few weeks, too, if you work or play as part of a team. There should be some sort of breakthrough or some good news. New pals you make during this time will influence your life in quite a spectacular fashion.

22 MONDAY Loved ones may want to lean on you but, frankly, you could do with a shoulder yourself to give you support. Make sure you are clear in asking for what is important. Mixed messages and crossed lines could have everyone off on a wild goose chase, which is less than useful. You have a lot on your plate at the moment and there is a good chance of your plans working out well, so stay organized and focused.

23 TUESDAY Reactions at home may take your eye off the ball at work or out in the community. Maybe you need to take a step backwards just for an hour or so to sort out misunderstandings, or at least disentangle your own thoughts. Then you will be off flashing your brilliance in all directions. However, you do have a soft approach because although the stars' influence will help to recommend you, certain companions are still being defensive.

24 WEDNESDAY Although you are thought of as a straightforward fire sign, you do have an interest in matters spiritual and even mystical. When you feel disinclined to settle down to chores, you often let your mind wander off to faraway places and fascinating speculations. Just remember to touch base every so often. You may travel in the wrong direction if you do not keep an eye on time and arrangements.

25 THURSDAY Venus will be moving into the airy sign of Gemini, throwing a happy and interesting glow over your friends and acquaintances. If you happen to be single, you may meet someone special while visiting a club or taking part in some sort of team effort. These are the avenues to try then if you are single but, if you already have a mate, you must try to behave yourself even though it may be difficult.

26 FRIDAY You may be slightly puzzled by the attitude of one friend or colleague. What they say and what they mean appear to be two different things. Being devastatingly honest and up-front yourself, you are sometimes confused by people cast in a different mould. They may be too timid or too confused to really know what they are trying to achieve, so be patient and forgiving and you will find they come round in time.

27 SATURDAY A peaceful and harmonious day thanks to the aspect between your ruling planet, the Sun and Uranus. You may have fallen out with somebody recently and so this is the time for making amends and also making a fresh start. Should you be single, keep a high profile this evening because it could be a wonderful one for new romances and all relationships.

28 SUNDAY For once, over a tiny trivial issue, you seem genuinely puzzled about what to do next. Sometimes just skipping over the question marks is the best way to proceed. Look kind, caring and all-knowing and then no one will guess that you have not the first idea, for the time being, about the answers. By next week you'll be back on top form again, shining a clear light on the way ahead. Why not relax and give in to temptation.

29 MONDAY It is possible that today you seem aloof and unapproachable to work colleagues. The time has therefore come for you to be less defensive. You understand wants and needs and by placing these centre stage you will be making new friends and associates. Also, you will derive a great deal of benefit from considering a career change.

30 TUESDAY Mercury moves into the watery sign of Cancer, and because of this there'll be a good deal of thinking and planning going on in the background, especially where financial matters are concerned. It could be that you're trying to decide whether or not you can afford to take a holiday. Just for once you're thinking first before plunging ahead.

31 WEDNESDAY Venus is in a beautiful aspect with Neptune. Therefore, you're at your most creative, so if you work in an area where you use your imagination you will be coming up trumps. This evening bodes well for romance too, so do get out and be ready to greet strangers with a smile on your face.

JUNE

JUNE IS DEFINITELY A MONTH when it's who you know that is really going to count. Should you have contacts abroad, they'll be in touch with you. Or it may simply be that you are planning your summer holiday and, of course, it'll be the most luxurious you can possibly afford or not afford. However, that won't deter you when it comes to spoiling yourself. You'll be meeting new friends of both sexes and team activity in your spare time is sure to be successful. Visits to clubs will offer you the opportunity for finding new romance, so make sure that you're looking your best and are out in the big wide world.

Unfortunately, Mercury will go into retrograde movement after the 23rd so it is not a good time as far as transport is concerned, which could let you down. It also is not a time for spending unnecessarily. You can always find an excuse to spoil yourself, but if you do so at this time you'll be counting the cost probably for the rest of the year. Take a persuasive friend with you when you go out shopping, or better still get somebody else to do it for you. Now look at the *Daily Guides* for further information.

1 THURSDAY June starts off in a difficult aspect between your ruler, the Sun, and Pluto. This seems to suggest that your progress may be blocked, either where a property matter is concerned or perhaps by a member of the family. Luckily, this is only for 24 hours, so don't get yourself all stressed out. The best thing to do is to really relax this evening.

2 FRIDAY Today is the day of the New Moon and it falls in the airy sign of Gemini. This is the area of your chart devoted to friendship, club activities and team effort, all of which can be lucky. Should you be single then get out this evening because there is a possibility of a new romance. I'm not saying it's going to be the love of your life, but it'll certainly do for the time being.

3 SATURDAY Jupiter is in a friendly aspect with Saturn, so opportunities that come your way in any area of life are likely to be lasting. Certainly, you may be suspicious of them initially, but having done your homework you will realize that this is the way to go. But please don't leave it too long because opportunities rarely come twice.

4 SUNDAY You feel envious of those who have developed skills that can make life easier and more pleasant. It's never too late to learn. With the stars today encouraging you to take the first lesson, you'll soon discover how powerful your newly gained knowledge has made you.

5 MONDAY Uncertainties about home, career or finances are disappearing one by one. You should

let it be known that it's not all your own work.
Acknowledge the importance of an unlikely connection and prove you would go to any lengths to
protect it. You are creating something wonderful, so
don't pretend otherwise.

6 TUESDAY Other people expect you to make decisions
for them. But you must not feel you are under
pressure or on the line. Insist on having the freedom to explore all options and to stop and start
again as often as you like. There may not be an
obvious choice but eventually you'll find one that
suits everybody's needs.

7 WEDNESDAY Just when you least expect it, a
change of circumstances will give you cause to
celebrate. The stars today are about to bring pleasing
news to your notice. You'll feel better about yourself
and an unusual situation. But most important of
all, you'll stop worrying so much and that's a very
good thing.

8 THURSDAY This is a great day for short trips,
shopping and outings. You are going to find it rather
hard to sit still for any length of time, so shelve any
intensive mental work for the time being. It is a
time, too, when you are likely to receive interesting
and important messages and mail. Be quick to reply,
otherwise there is a danger you may lose out.

9 FRIDAY Your need for a change of scene is obvious
and others are in the same position. Don't be

surprised if you stumble across a scheme or idea that suits everybody concerned. It might seem unusual or overgenerous on your part, but once you make up your mind your critics may as well save their breath.

10 SATURDAY Your ruling planet, the Sun, is lining up closely with Venus, so you are charm itself. This then is clearly an ideal day for getting whatever or whoever you want. Pull out all the stops and get cracking as soon as possible.

11 SUNDAY The Sun is a beautiful aspect with Uranus. Therefore, you have an ideal day for collecting favours from anybody, both at work and at home. This evening, if you are single, get out and about because there is a real chance of romance.

12 MONDAY A treat is coming your way even though you may not notice it at first. This is because it will arrive in disguise or under cover. Once you spot it, just a couple of tweaks will transform it into something tailor-made for your. Don't question it until you've tried it. It's worth more than you think.

13 TUESDAY High standards are called for in a busy area of your life. However, with the planets moving into a crucial position on your chart, you may push and shove to a point where companions feel threatened. Make allowances for those who cannot move at your speed. You'll achieve more and argue less.

14 WEDNESDAY A pat on the back may not be what you want, but you would probably like some recognition of the fact that you are making headway in a competitive and difficult area. Put others on the spot and ask for their reaction. If your talents or time are not fully appreciated, they may have to look elsewhere.

15 THURSDAY Your planet, the Sun, is lining up with Saturn. You've bags of concentration and should use it to either make decisions or perhaps turn your attention to intricate, problematic work. A person may have some good advice for you.

16 FRIDAY Today is the day of the Full Moon and it falls in the fiery sign of Sagittarius. This is not a good day for dealing with matters related to higher education or other countries because things could go awry. It might also be a good idea to get in an early night, especially if you're beginning to feel jaded. After all, you've been fairly busy lately.

17 SATURDAY Mars will be moving into the water sign of Cancer. Therefore, where your sex life is concerned there will be a tendency for you to be somewhat secretive. Perhaps you already have a mate but have developed a strong crush on somebody else. This, to me, seems as if you are courting danger and if you think anything of that special someone in your life, you'll exercise a certain amount of self-control.

18 SUNDAY Today seems to be a lucky one for you. One in which you'll find yourself in the right place at the right time, so be quick to say yes to all opportunities. This evening get out into the spotlight because that's where you belong. The more hectic your evening, the more you will enjoy yourself.

19 MONDAY Venus will be moving into the water sign of Cancer. It looks as if you are about to enter a phase where you'll be anything but honest where you love life is concerned. Actually, this probably won't apply if you don't have a mate. But if you do and you value the relationship, then you must fight against temptation, no matter how difficult.

20 TUESDAY At work you are in a helpful and cooperative mood for much of the day. You aren't selfish by nature and you will be seriously trying to help somebody else. Your own talents will be obvious and in your personal life you will be optimistic. This evening you may have to look after someone else's welfare or belongings, and this could make you anxious.

21 WEDNESDAY You must build on opportunities that come your way. If you let them pass you by, you may not get another chance. Be positive in your attitudes, especially towards those at work. If you are in a relationship, it is a slightly niggling evening. A trip out of the house will do you both good.

22 THURSDAY Today promises to be fuller, richer and more exciting, thanks to the astrological set-up being in a particularly useful area of your chart. You'll be free to pursue an idea that could boost your work or swell funds. If you leave others to fend for themselves more often, all well and good.

23 FRIDAY Mercury will be moving into retrograde movement, so wherever possible while this state of affairs exists avoid signing on the dotted line or making unnecessary trips. Paperwork could trip you up, so double-check it and don't be careless. Avoid expensive shops, you simply can't afford to go over the top right now.

24 SATURDAY You will have had to fight hard to reach your current position in life. You may feel there is someone who could have provided more help along the way. Without appearing vengeful or spiteful, let it be known that you're glad you can stand on your own two feet and you'll be doing more of it in the future.

25 SUNDAY Only you know how ambitious and determined you feel. The planetary movement today means that you'll get your side of the story across. You must be given the chance to prove your worth. You've said it before, now say it again. Only this time make it clear that you'll accept no compromises or half measures.

26 MONDAY You may be ready to blaze a trail through exciting new territory. Try not to be disappointed if you find you have to begin your journey alone. You'll be fine: you always are at a time like this. So don't make a fuss or insist on apologies or explanations. You won't get them, and you don't need them.

27 TUESDAY No one could accuse you of being ungenerous, so it seems unfair that you are being asked to contribute even more. Such demands usually mask something else entirely. Try letting others know how much they mean to you. By dealing in affection, not hard cash, everybody would be better off.

28 WEDNESDAY You feel tempted to curry favour with those in prominent positions. However, the starry set-up today means your heart is dictating your actions. If a relationship has more appeal than anything else, why worry about the future for the time being? Nothing matters more than the here and now.

29 THURSDAY There's work to be done and decisions must be made. A great deal is left up to you. The timing is unfortunate, however, as someone is about to spring a surprise that could provide a happy, healthy distraction from your busy schedule. If a little magic finds its way on the scene, enjoy every moment.

30 FRIDAY Jupiter will be moving into the airy sign of Gemini, throwing a glow over your friends and acquaintances for the remainder of the year. Quite clearly therefore it won't pay you to be too independent. If you think you need some kind of advice, take it from those you trust. They will not let you down. Teamwork is also well starred.

JULY

JULY IS A FAIRLY COMPLICATED MONTH, so let's take the negative first. Your ruling planet, the Sun, Mars and Mercury are all in a rather secretive part of your chart. This can mean either that you're busy studying for something special, or perhaps you're plotting and scheming in an effort to get even with somebody who may have upset you. Now this is all out of character. Naturally, nobody likes to be hurt, but as a Leo you have a big, warm generous heart and usually are prepared to put it down to somebody else's character faults and dismiss it from your mind, but not now. Perhaps this is a case of somebody trying to steal your mate away, in which case who can blame you for coming out fighting.

Venus will be in your sign from the 13th onwards and so after this you can do no wrong. You're looking good and feeling good, and you love the whole world. A wonderful time for making new partnerships, whether professional or personal. If you happen to be single, then you may just meet somebody who will stir those heartstrings of yours late month. If you've been in a relationship for some time, then some of you may even be marching up the aisle, and what a wonderful month you have chosen for doing just that.

Financially, don't make any major purchases until after the 17th, when Mercury resumes direct movement. To do otherwise would mean that you'll be well and truly ripped off. You don't mind giving your money away, but you hate to be conned. Now look at the *Daily Guides* for further information.

1 SATURDAY The month gets off to a promising start because there's a twinkling New Moon in the sign of Cancer. This perhaps isn't quite as important to you as it is to other people. But even so those instincts are extremely strong at this time and if you're wise you'll listen to them, even if you don't like what you hear. Work done behind the scenes may provide a breakthrough too.

2 SUNDAY Your planet, the Sun, is lining up with Pluto, and so you're in a mood for making changes. However, may I suggest that you wait a couple of days because the stars aren't exactly going to be helpful. In fact, you may find yourself blocked, so occupy yourself in some other direction.

3 MONDAY The Sun is lining up with Mars, and so your sex appeal is obvious to everybody around. Your energy knows no bounds and if you're taking part in anything physically strenuous, whether it be sex, sports or any kind of fun and games, you are sure to be doing exceptionally well.

4 TUESDAY Gradually you are seeing signs that your ideas are being accepted. Although circumstances may not be quite what you want, you can work to alter whatever you dislike later on. Family life may change as a result. Encourage others to let go of yesterday, because memories are holding everybody back.

5 WEDNESDAY A bout of bickering may erupt from a tiny incident, leaving you wondering whether a heart-to-heart discussion is called for. The planets right now are about to underline a crucial point. Focus on the relationship rather than the actual problem, which should soon be over and done with.

6 THURSDAY It appears you have less ready cash at your disposal than you're used to. But it is tempting to take an outside chance on something which could produce profit. Even if it doesn't, you won't regret having had a go. There are times in life when an element of risk works wonders. This is one of them.

7 FRIDAY Provocative comments may set your mind racing about property or long-term security. A conversation you instigate doesn't so much provide answers as raise more questions. There's no point in turning the clock back. You must have known change was in the air, so make it work in your favour.

8 SATURDAY Stories you have kept to yourself are being leaked. You'll be pleased because it means you are no longer sworn to secrecy. Even so, the planets' influences remind you that there's no need for everything to be revealed. Someone's pride is in the balance. What's left out is as important as what is left in.

9 SUNDAY You may have been struggling to handle some rather delicate issues, but your head is about clear and your spirits soar. Inspiration will arrive the minute you accept that anything no longer valid must be eliminated and replaced with something achievable. Prepare to make an impact that will last.

10 MONDAY You seem to be giving up on a much talked about project. That's a pity because you have it in you to create something unique. The planets are making you aware you are abandoning the idea for all the wrong reasons. You may not win prizes, but seeing it through to the end is a victory in itself.

11 TUESDAY Surprise events may start you wondering how you really feel about an intense relationship. It might be convenient to shift the blame on to an innocent bystander. The aspects today suggest, however, that if anyone is complicating things, you are. But stick with it and see what happens.

12 WEDNESDAY Your ruling planet, the Sun, is activated by chaotic Uranus, and so disorganization seems to be the theme of the day. However, there is a credit side to this because if anything or anyone pops up completely out of the blue, they are likely to be important to you for some time to come, so bear this in mind.

13 THURSDAY Venus will be moving into your sign, lucky you. This means that you will be looking and feeling your best over the next couple of weeks or so. Those of you in steady relationships may be preparing to make a decisions and if you have decided to become engaged or even married you have chosen a good time to do so. If you're single, you should keep a high profile.

14 FRIDAY A partner's plans continue to intrigue you and you'll no doubt have to provide support and backing. It may be hard to come up with the resources required, but do your best. You know you would be in good hands if the situation were reversed. If you can't provide a bit of magic at this time, then no one can.

15 SATURDAY Your money planet, Mercury, is activated by Pluto. This suggests that a sudden mood could ravage your bank account. Keep your hard-earned cash in the bank where it belongs. Opt for good company this evening rather than luxurious pastimes or surroundings.

16 SUNDAY Today is the day of the Full Moon and it occurs in the earthy sign of Capricorn. This suggests you may be lacking in energy, enthusiasm and the fire that you usually have. If so, then stick to routine things. You may not approve of the advice I'm about to give, but even so, an early night would work wonders for you. It might also be a good idea to temporarily ignore the telephone. After all, even you are not indestructible.

17 MONDAY Mercury finally resumes direct movement and so there is precious little to worry about with travelling and paperwork from now on. Finances, too, will be given a boost and will be a great deal easier. Cheques that have been delayed turn up and you begin to feel much more optimistic about the future.

18 TUESDAY It's said that out of failure comes success and the fact that you have not met all your targets recently should spur you on towards the achivements you deserve. No one could blame you for setting your sights high. After all, you can be both confident and competent. But make sure over the coming days that you don't push yourself to the point of exhaustion. Your health and well-being are just as important as success.

19 WEDNESDAY Something bubbling to the surface might put colour in your cheeks. Loved ones or colleagues should notice you're excited, embarrassed or both. Draw on your reserves of confidence and hope you can avoid making a full confession. You'll amuse everyone with the details one of these days.

20 THURSDAY Your ruling planet, the Sun, is lining up with Saturn. This increases your concentration making it far easier for you to deal with work that normally you would deem to be beneath you. The influence of an older person this evening is important. Perhaps you're receiving some words of advice. Whether you listen, of course, is entirely up to you but you should consider twice before you reject it.

21 FRIDAY The pressure is on to start solving problems between friends or at work. However, not everyone is as adaptable as you and any changes you suggest may need to be taken apart then put back together. Forcing the issue is a waste of time. Acquiring the patience of a saint is your only hope.

22 SATURDAY Conflict and confusion may leave you unsettled. That's a pity because you're facing challenges which would enhance your personal or professional reputation. This period of uncertainty will soon pass. When it does, you'll see the difference between what's worth worrying about and what is not.

23 SUNDAY The Sun moves into your sign and you begin your period of the year when you can push ahead with everything that is important to you. You're going to have increased confidence in yourself and your ideas. Physically, you will be blossoming, so make the most of this time because to waste it will lead to regret.

24 MONDAY Previous experience may not be much use to you today. You could be confronted by a new kind of situation, at work or in your personal life. You will be feeling your way and experimenting, not knowing quite what to expect. Whatever occurs will probably be of a temporary nature, so don't worry about the future too much. Other people may be in a competitive mood, but you must use your brain if you want to win. Encourage new acquaintances; they will be useful later.

25 TUESDAY There is a chance that there may be a cooling off period with a relative, friend or lover. This is mainly due to the fact that your mind appears to be on other matters. A time therefore for putting your wants and needs before those of your family and friends. Just for once it won't hurt for you to be a little bit selfish.

26 WEDNESDAY Keep a high profile today as it is an excellent time for looking for fresh outlets for your talents, especially if you are looking for a job. Those of you at work will be rushed off your feet from the moment you arrive to the moment you go home. Because of this you need to spend time this evening with those who are able to bring a smile to your face. It is not a time for romantic decisions.

27 THURSDAY Your ruling planet, the Sun, lines up with Neptune, and so you may not be as organized as you usually are. You may experience memory lapses, too, therefore refer to your diary and double-check all your arrangements otherwise you could finish up annoyed.

28 FRIDAY Your ruling planet, the Sun, lines up with Jupiter. You may experience, therefore, a certain amount of good luck. Certainly, you are feeling optimistic about the future and this is very attractive for everybody, including the opposite sex. Invitations for having fun seem to be pouring in.

29 SATURDAY Confidence should be your middle name today. Socially, romantically and in your family life you will quickly discover that others are willing to rally around and act upon your suggestions. This assertive manner is likely to attract the attention of the opposite sex. A new relationship could very well get off the ground. If you already have a partner, then they will be quite happy to back you up in all directions.

30 SUNDAY You are not exactly practical when it comes to money. However, you do like to know you have something saved away for those little occasions when you want to break out and be self-indulgent. This is one of those times. There is nothing wrong with this at all, providing you do not go completely over the top. Spoil yourself by all means, as it will certainly lift your spirits and a new possession will keep you busy. Well, for a couple of hours anyway.

31 MONDAY Today is the day of the New Moon and it falls in your sign. So you end this month on a high, feeling good, looking good and ready to make some important moves as well as decisions. Yes, this is a time for being a little bit cheeky and if you can't get away with it, then there's no hope for the rest of us.

AUGUST

WELL, LEO, WITH NO LESS than three planets in your sign this month, it's certainly your time of the year. You've extra confidence, warmth, generosity and attractiveness. Not only that, but your mind is full of bright ideas and your conversation is absolutely fascinating, so you're bound to be making new friends and contacts at a rate of knots. It's also a time for getting your own way, providing you turn on that fabulous, dazzling smile of yours. You can wrap the rest of us round your little finger if you so desire, and you probably won't even know that you're doing it.

Venus' placing in the financial area of your chart from the 7th onwards can't be bad news either. There's a suggestion that you're spending money on a few luxuries, but then you wouldn't be a Leo if you weren't. There's also a chance that money that is owed is coming in and will be more than you had expected. Regardless of your own sex, females will be particularly helpful when it comes to the practical side to life, so don't hesitate to ask them for some help if you sincerely believe that you need it.

Lastly, Pluto will be in retrograde action until the 20th. Therefore, do not make any important decisions until after this date, particularly if they're connected with creative work, social life or children. To do otherwise would be making life unnecessarily hard and that is the last thing that any normal Leo wants. Now look at the *Daily Guides* for further information.

1 TUESDAY This month starts off with Mars moving into your sign. Therefore, you have plenty of energy, sex appeal and initiative at your disposal over the next few weeks or so. Use them well. Regardless of your own sex, your male friends will be important. They'll be handing on useful tips and maybe opportunities, so shelve your pride and listen to what they have to say.

2 WEDNESDAY It is likely that one problem will disappear due to changed circumstances and a career question will be answered by advice from a couple of close friends. Avoid the urge to fret unduly about friends' troubles. There comes a point when you can't help any more. If there have been any romantic complications, especially if your mate has been too proud, then go for a happy reconciliation. Put the past behind you and be prepared to start all over again.

3 THURSDAY There is a chance you may step on other people's toes at work today. It is possible, too, that the negative feelings of other people may rub off on you. This is because you are a chameleon and tend to blend into your surroundings. However, fight for your own individuality and remember that you are always in control of your own fate.

4 FRIDAY Something will occur today which will give you plenty of food for thought. You will realize that the reason for living is to do something positive and of significance. Do your best to prove that the world would be a sadder place without you. Remember that you are original, there is only one you and that you are here to fill a certain need, either in the life of someone else or to contribute to the world in general. Let us not have any self-pity or doubt.

5 SATURDAY You seem to be giving up on a cherished project. This is a pity, because you have it in you to create something unique. The stars are making you aware you are abandoning the idea for all the wrong reasons. You may not win prizes, but seeing it through to the end is a victory in itself.

6 SUNDAY One of the important lessons to remember today is that everybody, including yourself, may outgrow places, hobbies and people. The thought of this may pull on your heartstrings, but be prepared to let go. It is possible that these aspects of life and their accompanying problems were relevant to a different stage of your development. Remember that life is about movement and is never the same from one day to the next.

7 MONDAY Mercury will be moving into your sign, enlivening your whole personality and allowing you to express yourself far more easily than is usually the case. Furthermore, you are extremely restless, so hopefully you have booked a summer holiday during this month. If you have, you have certainly picked the ideal time for doing just that.

8 TUESDAY Venus moves into the earthy sign of Virgo, and so over the next couple of weeks or so it's likely you'll be spending more money on luxuries and leisure-time activities rather than on necessities. Do ensure that you don't go completely over the top, otherwise you'll have to face the music at some point.

9 WEDNESDAY Surprise events may start you wondering how you feel about an intense relationship. It might be convenient to shift the blame on to an innocent bystander. But the stars suggest that if anyone's complicating things, you are. Stick with it and see what happens.

10 THURSDAY Saturn will be moving into the sign of Gemini, and because of this it's likely that certain friends and acquaintances won't be quite their easy-going selves. You may be gaining some responsibility through one of your contacts and although it may not seem to be a good idea at first, rewards will come at a later date – so be patient.

11 FRIDAY There is certainly a happy glow over all your associations and particularly friendships. Should you need any advice, help or encouragement then do not hesitate to go to those who are in the know and who care about you. It is a good time for the Leo who works as part of a team because there may be some good news.

12 SATURDAY Conflict and confusion may leave you unsettled, which is a pity because you're meeting challenges which could enhance your personal or professional reputation. A period of uncertainty will soon pass. When it does, you'll see the difference between what's worth worrying about and what is not.

13 SUNDAY One way or another you seem to feel tied down or hemmed in, or perhaps you are trying to preserve the peace. By doing so, the chances of making money are increased, despite the fact that you are not likely to receive anything before a decision is given. However, that doesn't mean that a promise won't be kept today.

14 MONDAY At times it's not easy for you to assert yourself or follow through with your actions. This is one of them. Don't imagine, however, that certain changes will make the slightest difference, in spite of having to do a bit of negotiating today. What occurs, once this week is over, ought to lead to greater happiness.

15 TUESDAY Today is the day of the Full Moon and unfortunately it falls in the partnership area of your chart. Don't be surprised, therefore, if other people are snappy, bad-tempered or simply dreamy. Best to leave them to their own devices and get on with your own business. They'll snap out of it in the near future and probably will be feeling fairly repentant.

16 WEDNESDAY Whether or not you are using the wrong approach, somehow you don't expect certain individuals to change their minds or take a stand today. Perhaps it's up to you to speak out, though don't be surprised if there is a power struggle now. In any event, knowing this will help you to determine what you want to achieve.

17 THURSDAY By nature you seldom give in, even though you cannot predict what the outcome of recent meetings or confrontations will be. This applies today, even if other people appear cold and calculating at first. Realistically, you are entitled to ask for more. In practice, your need for security is likely to affect your decision.

18 FRIDAY This is not a time to force the pace, especially as current aspects suggest that partners or employers effectively bar your way. Instead, you should return later and remember you have other matters to attend to today. In fact, you should make a lucky discovery which may be true or of no value at all.

19 SATURDAY Things are hotting up. A challenging aspect today denotes that your nearest and dearest are inclined to go on the rampage. Obviously, you will do better without them, but you mustn't let on or you could get yourself in some interesting situations between now and later in the week.

20 SUNDAY Pluto finally resumes direct movement which is good news, because no doubt family and property matters have been somewhat complicated and even stressed. Now that this has occurred the following days will ease past problems and you'll slowly begin to feel that you're getting back on top again.

21 MONDAY Your ruling planet, the Sun, lines up with Mercury. So if anyone can persuade other people into doing exactly what they want them to it is you. A good time for sorting out finances and money that is owed should roll in and if not, chase it.

22 TUESDAY Mercury moves into the financial area of your chart, and so over the next few weeks many of you will be gaining either through travel or by signing on the dotted line. Either way, it looks as if you're in for a profitable time but that doesn't mean you can spend on a promise, wait until everything has been put in writing.

23 WEDNESDAY The Sun will be moving into Virgo, emphasizing the cash area of life where, it has to be said, you are going to be far more canny and even quite tight. We all need a time of the year for using common sense, especially you because you can spend more money in half an hour than most people do in a week. This won't be the case over the next few weeks or so.

24 THURSDAY A tense link in the heavens implies that you may be denied access in some way. However, it makes sense to go through different channels, since you cannot trust everybody. The more unobtrusive you are, the better. It is probably hard to motivate yourself, but there is no need to stray too far today.

25 FRIDAY There is no point in complaining, particularly if no one wants to help out or work with you. Indeed, you probably won't know who to turn to today. However, just make the best of what you have, rather than doing something foolish. You should not think of yourself as a failure.

26 SATURDAY After all you have done for others, the tendency now is to brood or be seen but not heard. Just as well, for there are options you might not have even considered. In the meantime, a friend or close associate has found a remedy. But you know what they say Leo, only fools rush in.

27 SUNDAY Your ruling planet, the Sun, lines up with confusing Neptune. Therefore, it would not be a good idea for making important moves or decisions, because it's unlikely you have all the facts at your fingertips. You're in a romantic mood, too, so spend your time this evening with somebody you really care about and show them lots of affection.

28 MONDAY The planets today suggest that other people are waiting for some kind of feedback from you. They can see that you are preoccupied but refuse to leave you alone. How selfish of them. You are depending on other people's goodwill, whether you get anything out of it or not.

29 TUESDAY Today is the day of the New Moon and it occurs in the financial area of your chart. How useful, because this tends to suggest that either you will be receiving a long-awaited cheque or there will be a financial opportunity for you. But this does not mean putting your hard-earned cash at risk, that would be sheer foolhardiness.

30 WEDNESDAY A series of complex planetary aspects will allow you to prove just how self-sufficient or resourceful you are. Admittedly, you might still experience a few frustrations, due to the demands that are now being placed on you personally or at work. However, an invitation of some kind will lift your spirits.

31 THURSDAY It's important to keep things in perspective, no matter how difficult it is for you to explain your feelings or get your message across today. As long as you are honest with yourself, loved ones and co-workers will be more understanding. You may have to resort to various devices to gain self-respect. Venus' move into Libra suggests you are entering a couple of weeks when it will be a good idea to go travelling.

SEPTEMBER

FOR THE MOST PART during this month you'll be quite prepared to keep a low profile. Possibly you're making plans and certainly your attention is being taken up with financial matters. Where you would normally spend in order to spoil people you care about, now you think twice about it, with the exception of course of the odd day here and there that you can discover in the *Daily Guides*. It might also be a good idea to hang on to possessions, because Mars suggests that they could disappear and you may lose something valuable.

The placing of Venus and Mercury in Libra certainly makes you feel optimistic about life. You have good ideas and other people are prepared to listen. You'll meet new people who you find interesting and in some instances a casual romance may actually turn into something more important. However, don't go looking for it, just be happy that you are meeting new people who seem to like you. Then you'll be swelling your social opportunities as well as boosting that ego of yours, which, as a lion, invariably needs to be constantly fed. All in all September looks to be promising. Now look at the *Daily Guides* for further information.

1 FRIDAY Your ruling planet, the Sun, is activated by Jupiter, which could make you overoptimistic and perhaps a little bit careless. The best thing to do is avoid anything which demands a great deal of concentration or intricacy, otherwise you'll need to do tasks more than once and that will only make you hot under the collar.

2 SATURDAY The Sun is active again but this time it lines up with Pluto, which could make this a frustrating day. You could get the distinct feeling that you are blocked on all sides, particularly where family or property matters are concerned. Just try to bear in mind this is only a 24-hour period, surely you can keep your patience that long. If you're going to storm around with steam coming out of your ears, you are really not going to be very popular and it'll be your own fault.

3 SUNDAY Mercury continues in Cancer, so over the next couple of weeks there's likely to be many changes and a great deal of movement at your home. If you're looking for a new home, you are bound to be lucky. All kinds of contracts can be signed with alacrity, in the knowledge that you're doing the right thing.

4 MONDAY Venus today lines up beautifully with Neptune, giving a romantic and creative feel to this day. If you have your eye on someone special, but have lacked the courage to approach them, then this is the time for pushing ahead. After all, who can resist a warm, generous, lovely person like your good self.

5 TUESDAY Moneywise, the pressure should soon be off. But don't look for something else to worry about. Sometimes we must learn to leave well alone and not try to engineer everything towards a neat and tidy conclusion. In the words of the Chinese saying: When spring comes the grass grows by itself.

6 WEDNESDAY In spite of your reputation for being powerful and energetic, you have shown humility and caution in your dealings with someone in authority. Your tactics are likely to pay off, too, as you'll discover during the next round of talks. Little by little you are achieving more than you realize.

7 THURSDAY Some illuminating facts are about to come into your possession and you can walk away from those who have given you problems. It is not in your nature to be vengeful, but on this occasion you may consider reprisal. Do nothing until the middle of next week. Further details are yet to be revealed.

8 FRIDAY Your money planet, Mercury, is lining up with Saturn, which is good news because this will be applying a restraining influence on you. So when you pass those luxurious shops you'll realize that this isn't the time to splash out and make a big hole in your bank account. Concentration is good, too, so if you've intricate work to tackle you should have no difficulty whatsoever.

9 SATURDAY Mercury will be moving into Libra, stimulating those grey cells of yours and helping you to deal with work you normally find uncongenial. It's going to be a good few weeks for short trips and visits to friends and perhaps relatives. You'll be keeping on the go far more than usual.

10 SUNDAY Circumstances have forced you to neglect your routine obligations while you lend a hand elsewhere. Now you can reverse the trend, revert to type and show you are in control once more. Don't think your efforts are not appreciated. Although little is said, your generosity of spirit never goes unnoticed.

11 MONDAY Much of what you have been to scheming for will seem easier to attain soon. Even so, a personal involvement may become strained. Unless you clear up an unresolved mystery there will be more questions before you find any answers.

12 TUESDAY Saturn decides to go into retrograde movement, which suggests work may be less congenial to you than is usually the case. Furthermore, you might find that you are slowly running down. What needs to be done is for you to turn your attention to your physical well-being and pamper yourself as much as possible. This doesn't mean spending a great deal of money, far from it, it's those little pleasures that can make all the difference between optimism and pessimism.

13 WEDNESDAY Today is the day of the Full Moon and it occurs in the water sign of Pisces. This may herald some difficulty or problem in the life of somebody you are financially dependent upon. Ideally, this is not a day for reaching out into life, rather it is one for putting the finishing touches to work, or even relationships, before you move any further.

14 THURSDAY Your money planet, Mercury, is in a beautiful aspect with Jupiter. Therefore you may gain in some way, perhaps an overdue debt is finally paid, or maybe you are that lucky person who receives one of those tax rebates we all hear about. Either way this could be a happy day.

15 FRIDAY Venus is in a beautiful aspect with Uranus, and so people who are closest to you, both at work and at home, are loving, giving and ready to do your every bidding. If you have a secret crush on someone, now is the time for opening up and letting them know how you feel. Don't worry about hurt pride, it's most unlikely that they'll turn you down.

16 SATURDAY Mars is preparing to move into the earth sign of Virgo and so there may be setbacks, delays and perhaps older people seem to think they can boss you around. No doubt they will quickly discover that with a Lion that just isn't possible. But do keep a civil tongue in your head or you will be making enemies.

17 SUNDAY Mars is currently in the cash area of your chart and therefore it is not particularly good news. Because Mars encourages impulse and you have enough of this already, particularly when it comes to spending your hard-earned cash. The best thing to do is allow other people to do your important shopping and leave that money in the bank where it belongs.

18 MONDAY Mars is in a difficult aspect with Saturn, and so there is a stop/go feel about the day which you will find frustrating. Matters that you are perhaps waiting on in connection with higher education or from other countries may be delayed, so keep yourself busy in other areas because everything will come together.

19 TUESDAY Your money planet, Mercury, is busy with Uranus, so there may be a pleasant surprise where cash matters are concerned. However, on no account should you use this as an excuse to spoil yourself or other people, otherwise the damage you do will take a long time to repair. There is a romantic glow about the evening.

20 WEDNESDAY You have been talking at cross-purposes with someone who can influence business or property matters. The stars give you a clearer picture which can be easily seen. Watch carefully and be ready to revise your opinion on the way matters should be handled at this moment.

21 THURSDAY A series of mishaps and misunderstandings indicate you may have lost faith in someone's ability. Now, with all the extra duties you've taken on, it's essential that you have complete faith in yourself. You are the one about to be hurled into the spotlight. Be ready to perform on cue.

22 FRIDAY A creative, romantic or family affair has taken up time and you may be accused of pushing other pressing matters to one side. Don't overreact to what sounds like unfair criticism. The planets will enable you to focus on a scheme that dispels the doubts of the past few weeks.

23 SATURDAY The Sun will be moving into the air sign of Libra, and so from now on your mind will be firing on all cylinders as will your imagination. Furthermore, there will be many opportunities for you to take short trips or pay visits, both in your private life and professional life. So if you've any sense at all you'll pick up on this.

24 SUNDAY You may feel inclined to throw the rule book at someone whose behaviour seems to be out of character. But before your vent your anger, you must take into account certain facts that have so far been denied you. Until you have heard both sides of the story, you will be unwise to terminate any sort of agreement.

25 MONDAY Venus will be moving into Scorpio. This is the area of your chart devoted to home, family and property, where there is a rosy glow. It might be that you'll be entertaining your friends far more than you usually do. They will be completely spoiled because you are one of the best hosts/hostesses of the zodiac.

26 TUESDAY the Sun lines up with Neptune, so you are in an inspired mood and should put any ideas down on paper before you forget them. There's a romantic feel about the evening, too, therefore, if you are single, keep a high profile. You're looking good and somebody will be noticing.

27 WEDNESDAY Today is the day of the New Moon and it falls in the sign of Libra. This will be encouraging you to constantly keep on the go, while you do so you may be picking up on interesting information, as well as possible admirers for the future. Make a note of all your inspirations, you may be able to put them into use in the future.

28 THURSDAY Mercury is now moving into Scorpio and you should heave a sigh of relief because this means that those who are closest to you are finally being less awkward, stubborn and perhaps elusive. From now on, there'll be more peace and harmony between yourself and other people.

29 FRIDAY Mercury will be moving into the water sign of Scorpio. This will most certainly be livening up matters related to property, family and your home. Uncharacteristically, you will prefer to invite your friends to your home, rather than going out to some glitzy nightclub or restaurant. Think of the money you will be saving.

30 SATURDAY Jupiter goes into retrograde movement, which means that you could be in for a couple of weeks when confusion may reign where love affairs, social life, sports and artistic endeavours are concerned. Bear this in mind, double-check everything you are told and then you should be able to sidestep any problems the stars are laying out for you.

OCTOBER

UP UNTIL THE 23rd the Sun will be moving along in the air sign of Libra. This is the area of your chart devoted to the mind, which is going to be a great deal more creative, and also to short trips, as well as matters related to brothers and sisters. You're likely to be on the go from morning till night. But, if you are to make the most of this time, you will need to get yourself highly organized so that you don't run around in circles, which is a distinct possibility.

From the 23rd the Sun will be moving into the water sign of Scorpio. You have an ideal period then for talking through things with your flatmates or family. If you decide to throw a small party for your friends, you can be quite sure that it will go with a swing. There's a likelihood that during this latter part of the month you'll be reluctant to stray too far away. Either you're not feeling adventurous, or possibly you have met someone who is taking up all of your time and attention at home.

Unfortunately, Mercury is in an awkward mood and from the 18th onwards it will be moving into retrograde action, which means from our position in space it seems to be going backwards. While this state of affairs exists it would not be a good idea to tackle unnecessary travelling and don't sign important documents. All paperwork needs to be scrutinized carefully, because you will overlook something important if you only glance at it. Should you have a Gemini or Virgo in your life then you'll be making progress with them. Though this may be extremely difficult as they are hopping from one place to the other and don't seem to have a great deal of time for you, which might be a little bit hurtful.

Venus will also be in Scorpio up until the 18th, so there's a suggestion here that when it comes to having fun you may prefer to stick very close to your base. Perhaps you're giving dinner parties, or just having a good gossip with those in your intimate circle. From the 19th onwards, this planet moves into the fun area of your life, namely into the sign of Sagittarius. This will bring plenty of opportunities for romance which should perhaps not be taken too seriously. You're at your most flirty and so are other people. Mind you, if you happen to be involved in the arts, you'll have a lot of good ideas which will impress other people.

Regrettably, Mars will be situated in the sign of Virgo for this entire period, making you even more rash and impulsive when it comes to your hard-earned cash. You could become drawn to something in a shop window and rush in and purchase it without any clear thought of whether you can really afford to do so. If you give in to this mood, I'm afraid there could be some disagreements either with those closest to you or those who have an interest in your earning power and how you spend your money.

Mercury goes into retrograde movement on the 18th. While this state of affairs exists you'd be most unwise to take unnecessary trips or to sign documents. Make excuses to delay things and wait for a better time or you may be

Daily Guide – October

kicking yourself for the rest of the year. Now look at the *Daily Guides* for further information.

1 SUNDAY Your money planet, Mercury, is in a difficult aspect with Neptune. This suggests that either you will be careless, or that other people may try to detach you from your hard-earned money. Be alert to dubious characters.

2 MONDAY No one can deny you have been put through your paces at home. However, you must not think about what has been lost or sacrificed. Concentrate on what has been saved as a replacement. Very soon you will realize that recent trials were only leading towards something more worthwhile.

3 TUESDAY Pluto is in a friendly mood, so don't be surprised if you experience an almost manic desire to make changes simply for the sake of it. You need to make a list of all the alterations needed, then read it through several times just to make sure you are on the right track.

4 WEDNESDAY Mars and Pluto are in a difficult aspect and there's a certain amount of tension and explosion about this day. But you need to be particularly careful when in the company of acquaintances, strangers or people that you deal with, otherwise you could push them too far and an almighty explosion could result.

5 THURSDAY You seem to have a message to get across and will not be thwarted in your attempt to do so. You must have everyone's undivided attention. Very soon you'll have an audience which is ready and waiting for all of your pearls of wisdom, but it doesn't happen to be today.

6 FRIDAY Outside pressures have forced you to concentrate on serious issues, and there hasn't been much time for frivolity or fun. However, the planets today see common sense once more and will be opening up a new episode in your personal life. Be ready to write the first crucial words.

7 SATURDAY Your motto should be 'expect the unexpected' as you find it impossible to stick to any sort of schedule today. Don't let any last-minute changes throw you into confusion. Just lie back and enjoy the ride that the planets are planning for you. Who knows, if you can unwind a little you could even find some unexpected romance heading your way.

8 SUNDAY You're in a forgetful mood and if you don't make a note of anything important it's likely to slip your mind. Don't be too quick to judge a new person in the workplace as nerves are likely to be behind any arrogant behaviour that they show.

9 MONDAY Money matters are prominent today as you try to solve a longstanding problem between those closest to you. But try not to get too involved. They must sort out their differences and you must tell them that you are no longer willing to play piggy in the middle.

Good news concerning your finances reaches you very soon, allowing you to make some extravagant plans for the coming days.

10 TUESDAY Your ruling planet, the Sun, lines up with Uranus. You've bags of magnetism and charisma. Clearly this is the day for making all important moves, whether connected with the family, work or your romantic life. If you already have a partner, you'll need to control that flirty behaviour.

11 WEDNESDAY You are judging how your life is progressing by looking at the reaction of someone close. If you continue to rely heavily on the support of others, you will end up sorely disappointed. Trust your own judgement and make your own decisions. Time spent with a young person today should prove just how knowledgeable you really are, and your words of wisdom astound even you.

12 THURSDAY Every day brings something different for you during these times. You seem to be speaking without thinking and if you're not careful you will upset somebody who is relying on you for support at this time. Be careful what you say to a loved one, even in jest, because your sense of humour is likely to be a little extreme.

13 FRIDAY Today is the day of the Full Moon and it occurs in the fiery sign of Aries. Because of this you must stick to the letter of the law and, if it is necessary for you to travel from place to place, either during the day or during the evening, then drive a touch slower and whatever you do, don't drink and drive.

14 SATURDAY Mars is lining up with Uranus, so you can expect a lively and interesting day. Certainly, other people are bursting with energy and will have plenty of ideas for you to consider. This evening could be excellent for romance, so if you are single, spruce yourself up and get out into the big wide world.

15 SUNDAY Neptune finally resumes direct movement, which means people who you are financially dependent upon will emerge from a rather sticky phase. Mars also suggests that you must be careful where official matters are concerned. If you take any kind of risk or try to pull the wool over somebody's eyes, you will be caught out, if not today, then soon.

16 MONDAY Neptune continues in your opposite sign of Aquarius and, while this state of affairs exists, you may find yourself loaded down with extra responsibility and a heavy load of work. Simply resign yourself to the task at hand and minimize the moaning, then you'll gain a certain amount of respect.

17 TUESDAY You may suspect that someone is being anything but straightforward with you. If this is so, this would be the right time for a confrontation. However, make sure you remain calm, logical and fair-minded. It is a good time, too, for finding an outlet for one of your pet inspirations. You will discover that other people are extremely receptive to you right now. This evening give time to that special someone in your life.

18 WEDNESDAY Unfortunately, Mercury goes into retrograde movement. While this state of affairs exists I'm afraid there could be complications and difficulties where paperwork and finances are concerned. How difficult this is very much depends on you. If you insist on carrying on in a rather cavalier fashion and spending as if you're a millionaire, then you'll be letting yourself in for a good deal of stress. But if you can draw in your horns for the time being then all should be well.

19 THURSDAY Venus will be moving into the fiery sign of Sagittarius. This is the enjoyable part of your chart and it throws a glow over matters related to social life, romance and creative projects. Should you be a parent, then you will find that children will be excelling in all of their efforts and they'll be a joy to spend time with. Sports are lucky too.

20 FRIDAY Use the day ahead to think about how you are going to tackle your career. So many new paths are now open to you that if you don't take care when considering your choices you may miss out on some golden opportunities. The demands of a loved one take up some of your time this evening. During the coming days, it's important that you indulge not only their whims and wishes but also your own.

21 SATURDAY Venus is in a friendly aspect with Neptune, and because of this there's a certain amount of goodwill and friendliness at work. This might be an ideal evening for mixing business with pleasure, either so that you can pick other people's brains, or perhaps because you happen to have a strong attraction for someone. This is a day of action.

22 SUNDAY Your ruling planet, the Sun, is in touch with Saturn. This is a warning from the stars to take things a little bit slower and a little bit more carefully. Older people will have some good advice for you, but the problem is you're unlikely to listen to anyone at the best of times and so certainly not today – you could regret it.

23 MONDAY The Sun will be moving into the water sign of Scorpio. This is the area of your chart devoted to home, property and family matters. Now, this may not exactly fill you with excitement but there's a chance that you'll want to entertain at home far more during the coming weeks and will be doing so with your usual gusto. Make sure you notice if a loved one seems to be in pain or is in dire need of discussing matters with you.

24 TUESDAY Faces from your past come flooding back into your life as you attend some sort of event or gathering that reunites everybody. Resist the temptation to embroider the truth about your current situation or you could end up looking foolish. A romantic surprise awaits you and this should make up for a small hiccup you have encountered recently.

25 WEDNESDAY The stars today highlight your relationships and you should finally pluck up the courage to make someone know how you feel. Don't be afraid to introduce the person you care for to friends and family. If close ones don't accept them, that's their problem, but you can no longer go on living two separate lives. Watch out for an argumentative person who is determined to get a reaction from you, no matter what it takes.

26 THURSDAY Uranus resumes direct movement, and so any problems you may have had with other people, either at work or in your private life, begin to slowly melt away. You will wonder how you could have allowed your relationship to deteriorate to this stage, but at least somebody is waking up and hopefully it is you.

27 FRIDAY This is the day of the New Moon and it occurs in the home area of your chart. There could be some good news, or perhaps an extra activity resulting from entertaining with new friends. If you're looking for a new house or flat, this is the day to step up your efforts because you could be lucky. As always with New Moons, it's a time for making fresh starts.

28 SATURDAY Venus and Pluto are in fine form and if you need a time for mixing business with pleasure there really couldn't be a better one. Instead of approaching people during the working day, arrange to have a drink with them after hours. In this way you'll be a good deal more successful and lucky.

29 SUNDAY You may not be seeing eye to eye with a close one and you may actually be in the wrong place at the wrong time. Try to be thoughtful with a friend, problems with somebody could be blown out of all proportion. If you're working on this Sunday, keep an eye on fine details and you will be in for a pleasant surprise when your recent hard work is rewarded by a superior.

30 MONDAY You need to stop getting involved in everybody else's life and start sorting out your own. Could it be that you are so nervous of dealing with your own problems that you are using the worries of those close to you as an escape from what should really concern you? Don't be afraid to ask a new acquaintance for a date.

31 TUESDAY In an ideal world, you would like to put your feet up and let someone else take care of important business. But this is not an ideal world and you have been left in charge once more because you're the best person for the job. However, don't assume anyone is taking advantage of you. Just be proud of all you can do.

NOVEMBER

THIS MONTH THE SUN continues its progress through Scorpio until the 20th, placing the emphasis on family, activities at home and those people you live with. There may, of course, be some kind of reason why you are unwilling to go further afield, maybe you are involved in some kind of home study, in which case the stars will be helping you out by increasing your concentration.

From the 21st onwards the Sun will be moving into the fiery sign of Sagittarius. You will throw off the mantle of responsibility and hard graft and concentrate on getting maximum enjoyment out of your life. This part of November is particularly good for those professionally involved with children or the arts, that brain is in a positive and productive whirl.

Up until the 9th Mercury is moving through Libra. This gingers up the old grey matter and gives you plenty of good ideas, so do jot them down. It is also a time when you'll be bumping into interesting new people who will become fast friends and in some instances passionate lovers. Mercury moves into the water sign of Scorpio on the 9th, increasing activity at home and also helping those who are perhaps flat-or house-hunting. If you're exchanging contracts during this period, you've certainly picked a good time. There's going to be plenty of movement and news within the family or amongst your flatmates. Some of you may even decide to spruce up the old homestead, perhaps with an eye to the festive season. But if you do, do take things carefully, because you're in so much of a hurry you could make a mistake.

Venus continues to wend its way through Sagittarius

up until the 12th. So there's a great deal of fun and casual romance to be found during the first half of the month. Don't take any of it seriously though, simply let off steam. From the 13th onwards, Venus will be moving into Capricorn and the emphasis shifts to sheer hard work. Mind you, if you're involved in a professional partnership, or the arts, then you may be so engrossed by your work that you may forget to have sometime off to relax.

Mars will be entering the air sign of Libra on the 4th. This is the area of your chart devoted to the mind, which may be whirling around like a spinning top, so try to slow your thought process down. Otherwise mistakes could be made, and when somebody points this out you could fly completely off the handle. Furthermore, take a certain amount of care when travelling as minor accidents and prangs may occur, not to mention hot words exchanged.

If you can coast along and refuse to be ruffled, even by the most obnoxious people, then November could be an enjoyable time. Lastly, this placing of Mars suggests that you may be a little more sexually promiscuous than is usual. There appears to be a stream of admirers whose attentions are anything but honourable. Now, of course, they don't always have to be, but just make sure that you don't mistake an infatuation for something more serious. Now look at the *Daily Guides* for further information.

1 WEDNESDAY You're ahead in a crucial race and must let your prowess and expertise show. Even though friends and loved ones see you are forging ahead of them, they are happy for you to succeed. If waiting for hostile remarks or critical comments to bring you down a peg or two, relax because you're waiting in vain.

2 THURSDAY It's not how much you do for a loved one that counts but how readily you provide backup where it's needed most. The stars are encouraging you to show you are happy to be leaned on until this brief spell of confusion is over. Doing so, you'll strengthen a bond that means more to you each day.

3 FRIDAY Your ruling planet, the Sun, is in aspect with Pluto, and so you're in a restless and changeable frame of mind. You may even act out of character and deliberately block somebody else's progress, perhaps out of envy. By the time the evening arrives you'll wonder what on earth is going on inside that brain of yours. Don't worry, we all act out of character from time to time.

4 SATURDAY Mars will be moving into the airy sign of Libra. This will not only be speeding up your brain cells, which could be a good thing, it also will make you more impatient, particularly when travelling from place to place. If you are doing the driving, then either calm down or get somebody else to take the wheel.

5 SUNDAY Unless you keep on the right side of a partner or a loved one, you may start a battle of wits or words that will be difficult to bring to an end. Such arguments are time-wasting and exhausting, and are best avoided if possible. You'll have a chance to get your point across sooner than you think.

6 MONDAY Business or money ventures have hit a low through lack of drive and initiative. However, the stars will help you to come up with inspired ideas. Make certain they are practical, workable and affordable. If dealing with anything 'pie in the sky', you'll only add to your problems not ease them.

7 TUESDAY Time and time again you've given way to those who insist there's only one way to get things done – their way. However, by taking the line of least resistance, you do everybody a disservice. Your razor-sharp mind will come up with a new slant on an old problem. Find the courage to insist it is adopted.

8 WEDNESDAY Fortunately Mercury, your money planet, has decided to see sense and resume direct movement. So where you may have felt as if you were hitting your head up against a brick wall, now that wall caves in you can push ahead. Furthermore, it's a good time for dealing with legal matters and foreign affairs, so make sure you lay down your plans carefully.

9 THURSDAY Mercury will be moving into the watery sign of Scorpio, and this will be bringing many minor changes in connection with the family and property. If you're looking for a new home, then the next few days or so is the time to really step up your efforts.

There's a bargain waiting for you somewhere out there. Those waiting on news from abroad should not be disappointed.

10 FRIDAY That fiery planet, Mars, is lining up with Neptune. Therefore you may be receiving news from another country or in connection with education that you were expecting, but the contents may be quite surprising. This evening make sure you get out and about if you happen to be single. There's something irresistible about you at this time, so don't sit at home wasting it.

11 SATURDAY Today is the day of the Full Moon and unfortunately it occurs at the zenith of your chart. On the credit side this makes it an ideal time for putting the finishing touches to work. But if you try to be too adventurous, I'm afraid you will find yourself running into the proverbial brick wall. Workmates may be a little bit tetchy, too, therefore get out the olive branch and see what you can do to calm them down.

12 SUNDAY Hard work is on the agenda for this particular day. What you must not do is create such a song and dance that the atmosphere becomes tense. No one is making impossible demands. You're simply being asked to show yourself off at your brightest. It won't be difficult and the rewards will make it worthwhile.

13 MONDAY Venus will be moving into the earthy sign of Capricorn. This will throw a happy glow over routine work matters as well as your relationships with a colleague. Mind you, there might be a tendency for you to mix business with pleasure, and when you do you could go completely over the top, which will affect your health.

14 TUESDAY Your family matters must be handled one step at a time. True, it seems important to set the wheels in motion. However, you might jeopardize all the advantages you have unless you take someone's track record into account. Think about what you are trying to do. The best person to help you is close by.

15 WEDNESDAY Because your money planet, Mercury, is in touch with Neptune there could be a certain amount of muddle about possessions as well as finances, so avoid the expensive shops as well as luxurious entertaining. The ideal thing to do is to spend your evening at home kicking around doing little jobs you've neglected for some time, at least you'll stay solvent.

16 THURSDAY Financial matters should be brought to completion. Although you feel tempted to experiment, you must show you have every intention of keeping promises made some time ago. You're not merely dealing with current transactions; your reputation could be affected by what you do next. Do it well.

17 FRIDAY By behaving cautiously with those in authority, you are unlikely to put a foot wrong. But you may be missing out in terms of creative fulfilment and this could cost you dearly. You don't have to be rash or reckless. Just be yourself and don't let hidden fears mask your true talents.

18 SATURDAY One minute you're full of high hopes, the next your expectations fall to an all time low. However, don't think this period of uncertainty will last long. Business or legal matters should soon be settled to your satisfaction. Remember that at times like this a lot depends on how much cooperation you can expect from friends and associates. Make this the point at which you start to build up a rapport with those you don't know nearly well enough.

19 SUNDAY Unfortunately your ruling planet, the Sun, is in a difficult aspect with Saturn. Therefore, for reasons that you don't quite understand, you may either feel rather depressed or perhaps simply overburdened. Should anybody else try to add to your load, smile sweetly and say 'no'. It's not a time to take on more than you can comfortably handle.

20 MONDAY What seems a straightforward idea promises to liven up your social life. Unless you check out practicalities, however, you may encounter insurmountable problems or upset someone whose help you need. Look again at what's on offer. You might be expected to provide far too much in return.

21 TUESDAY Although the stars are shining on your creative streak, you may feel weighed down by administrative or relationship problems. But surely these can wait until you have achieved something you have put off for too long already? Make it clear you're not at everybody's beck and call.

22 WEDNESDAY The Sun will be moving into the fiery sign of Sagittarius. Luckily for you this is the area of your chart devoted to children, social life and casual romance. It looks as if you'll be attending many social occasions, or at least making up reasons for enjoying yourself. Things have not been easy lately and you could do with a couple of days or so for really letting that tension flow away.

23 THURSDAY You have been sitting on your laurels, it's time to get up and show yourself off in the best possible light. The planets today will provide you with whatever it takes to promote those thoughts and ideas that you have been reluctant to expound. So be as impulsive as you like. You can't lose.

24 FRIDAY Take things as slowly as possible. News that comes your way concerning your romantic interests should not be acted upon immediately. There is much more for you to learn before the day is over. Someone you met last week will prove that you made the right decision concerning a relationship. You should be able to sail through work matters with little or no effort at all.

Daily Guide – November

25 SATURDAY Today is the day of the New Moon and it falls in the fiery sign of Sagittarius. It looks as if there is either going to be an exciting new romance or a glamorous occasion for you to look forward to. Either way your spirits are high and you're bound to use this as an excuse to spend some money. Just as long as you don't go over the top.

26 SUNDAY This is an excellent day for paying visits, especially to relatives. This might not seem very exciting, but in doing so you might meet someone of importance. Ideas abound, too, so be sure that you jot them down in case you forget them. The telephone is likely to be white hot with people clamouring for your company.

27 MONDAY Don't be afraid to act on impulse and move off in a direction that has beckoned for some time. It's all too easy to come out with excuses to remain where you are. However, on this occasion, you risk losing all credibility with those whose opinions count for a lot. Stop weighing up the odds and just say 'yes'.

28 TUESDAY Your ruling planet, the Sun, is lining up with Jupiter, and so you're in a happy-go-lucky mood. But it is not an ideal day for dealing with detailed work, because you're likely to be too carefree and slapdash. Certainly, throw yourself into the social whirl this evening, but don't make it too much of a late night because you will run completely out of steam.

29 WEDNESDAY An important relationship may be flagging and left you wondering what the outcome will be. Since the stars are joining forces, you should see a way to put things on a firmer footing. First, however, you must make sure that a partner or loved one knows what you expect in return.

30 THURSDAY Now is the moment to reawaken those creative or artistic talents which for some time you have put to one side. Little can be achieved, however, without patience. If you give yourself a hard time in the early stages, you stand to learn nothing and your rewards will be few. Time is on your side, so use it well.

DECEMBER

DURING DECEMBER THE SUN will be moving through the fiery sign of Sagittarius up until the 21st. Fortunately for you this is the area of your chart devoted to the arts, matters related to children, casual romance and socializing. You're determined to extract the maximum amount of fun out of life, and even if invitations don't come your way you'll be sending them out yourself.

From the 21st onwards the Sun will be moving into the earthy sign of Capricorn. Therefore, it's very much a case of head down in order to finish projects before the festive period really gets cracking. Workmates will be helpful but don't take on too much and share your load. You don't want to begin Christmas completely out of sorts and suffering from stress.

Mercury is sailing through the fire sign of Sagittarius between the 4th and 22nd. This will continue to spice up your social life, bringing new people and perhaps inclining you to spare-time activities which could be classed as intellectual rather than simply frivolous. However, whatever you are doing new faces will be appearing and though nobody is going to be the love of your life, not for the time being, you'll be enjoying yourself anyway.

Venus enters your opposite sign of Aquarius on the 8th. This really is very good news because it's throwing a happy glow over the people closest to you, as well as providing chances for romance and flirting if you happen to be single. All kinds of partnerships thrive during this time and quite frankly you couldn't have a better gift for Christmas from the stars.

Mars, not surprisingly, will be in Scorpio late month, so there's a great deal of activity going on at home. It looks as if you are going to be acting the role of host/hostess over the festive period. Mind you, when people fail to jump when you tell them to, you could become snappy and bad-tempered. This is no way to behave, particularly during the holiday period. You don't want to begin that on bad terms with somebody. Remember that nobody is perfect and that includes you.

The pattern the stars are making throughout this month seems to suggest that you're not entirely in control of your own life. Just for once you need to listen to what other people have to say and even act on their advice. Even if it does go against the grain it will be the best thing for you, so pocket your pride. December throws down a challenge, but it's nothing that you cannot comfortably cope with. Now look at the *Daily Guides* for further information.

1 FRIDAY However long-suffering you may be, even you can't continue to tolerate the threats and insinuations of a certain person. You must, therefore, put inhibitions aside and speak out as you have rarely done before. This is your chance to take the floor, deliver a stunning speech and earn a standing ovation.

2 SATURDAY Mars is in a beautiful aspect with Uranus, and this will certainly liven up everybody who is closest to you, both at work and maybe even friends abroad who will be getting in touch. The stars are giving you the green light to do as you wish when it comes to your social life. You can even push ahead with a romance that you have so far hoped would blossom all on its own. This won't happen, Leo, it needs a little bit of effort.

3 SUNDAY Think hard before refusing to cooperate on a project that means a great deal to many people. The fact that you have been invited to join in is a compliment in itself. If you are prepared to sacrifice a little of your time, you'll almost certainly reap rewards which at this stage remain unseen.

4 MONDAY Mercury will be moving into the fiery sign of Sagittarius. This will certainly be livening up the family, particularly if there are youngsters amongst them. You may also be drawn to intellectual pastimes rather than physical ones over the next few weeks. This could mean that you are learning a new skill. Social occasions are prone to minor adjustments and changes, so do some double-checking.

5 TUESDAY For reasons you find hard to explain, you have been unable to get to grips with financial or property arrangements. Now, however, the planets are providing the confidence to face adversity. The mists are about to clear and everything will fall into place. Fear is your only stumbling block.

6 WEDNESDAY It seems you have been cast in the supporting role for too long and are ready to take centre stage. A rare opportunity to exploit your hidden talents must not go to waste. Therefore, do whatever is necessary to overcome a tendency towards shyness or diffidence. The next few days or so should see you moving onwards and upwards in a rather different world from the one you know.

7 THURSDAY There is work to be done and duties to fulfil, and the lion's share has been left to you. This shouldn't present a problem because the planets are providing all the energy and drive you need. Make it clear that this is an exception, not the rule, and refuse to carry those who can fend for themselves.

8 FRIDAY Venus will be moving into your opposite sign of Aquarius, which is good news because it throws a happy, harmonious and loving glow over all existing relationships. If, on the other hand, you are single, then make sure you're looking and feeling great over the next few days. Accept all invitations to enjoy yourself because that is the way you might meet that very special person.

9 SATURDAY At last you can fulfil a burning desire to confront issues that have led to frustration in the past. A sudden change of circumstances means you can persuade others to your way of thinking. Take the initiative and the risks should provide a happier, healthier lifestyle for all concerned. Think clearly and act fast.

10 SUNDAY Jupiter and Neptune are now in action, so it looks as if chances to have fun are coming in from everywhere and you are probably spoiled for choice. Look carefully through the ones you accept because if you try to cram everything and everyone in, it could throw a blight over any occasion simply because you are tired.

11 MONDAY Today is the day of the Full Moon and it occurs in the air sign of Gemini. This is a warning to be very careful when handling acquaintances and friends, because if you come on too strong I'm afraid somebody could exit stage left from your life, perhaps for ever. Teamwork should be set aside for the time being, whether it be professional or personal.

12 TUESDAY That money planet of yours is in action again and with Pluto this time. Therefore, it's likely that you have ignored advice to draw up a budget and be sensible and have decided to splurge instead. It isn't too late, if you've further shopping to do, but from how on hunt around for bargains. If you don't you're going to start next year in a very poor state.

13 WEDNESDAY You're about to see the light over an issue that has caused confusion. Although you may be relieved to clarify the matter, you realize it has taken on a greater importance than you first thought. What matters now is not so much that an error of judgement has been made, as how you intend to deal with it. Keep it simple.

14 THURSDAY A sudden change to financial arrangements is not nearly so dramatic as it first appeared. The stars indicate it's time to forget about set patterns or routines and allow innovative thinking to be the order of the day. Expect the unexpected and all will be well.

15 FRIDAY Mars and Saturn are in operation today, and so there could be a stop/go feel to everything. You need to double-check all your social arrangements in order to avoid disappointment at a later date. It could be, too, that you'll be dealing with somebody from a foreign country in some way.

16 SATURDAY You have more going for you than you would ever have thought, though perhaps not in the areas you might expect. Although you are seen as a fairly forthright person, your subtle powers could place you in a different league. Surprising news is on its way. Act on it with all the speed and enthusiasm you can.

17 SUNDAY As the Moon is in Virgo this is an ideal time for doing your Christmas shopping, even though it is a Sunday. However, just for once, do a little bit of budgeting and find out exactly how much you can afford to spend before you leave. Then you are unlikely to go over the top and have to pay the price at a later date.

18 MONDAY You might think shared responsibilities are weighing too heavily when all you really need is a little bit more fun. What you cannot see is how the benefits you are gaining will soon lead you to a happier, more fulfilling lifestyle. Be ready for a chance encounter to open the door to new possibilities.

19 TUESDAY Venus and Pluto and are in action today, so there's a strong possibility that you'll be mixing business with pleasure. It's the right time of the year for doing so, but often many of us make complete fools of ourselves. We're either overimbibing or chasing the opposite sex when we should be behaving ourselves. See if you can ensure that this year you will remain unscathed and free from guilt.

20 WEDNESDAY If you flex your muscles in the wrong areas you may alienate those whose help you need. Take note of feedback coming your way and you'll realize how close you have come to disrupting a workable and profitable arrangement. By appealing to someone's better nature you can repair the damage.

21 THURSDAY After recent ups and downs it may seem unfair that you are facing another battle. This time, however, the advantages are all yours and the fact that you are fighting on home ground guarantees success. The aspects from the stars today empowers you to assume your rightful place.

22 FRIDAY The Sun will be moving into Capricorn, so you may become a little overanxious about people you are financially dependent upon. It's possible that secretly they're doing quite well for themselves. They are afraid to admit it to you for fear that you'll help them to spend when they should be saving, and they are right.

23 SATURDAY Mercury joins the Sun in Capricorn, so there's likely to be some kind of celebration going on at work. Naturally, as a Leo, when you decide to have fun you throw caution to the wind. But it might be a good idea to keep one little toe on the ground, otherwise you could have cause for regret. That would be a pity and may spoil your Christmas.

24 SUNDAY Mars will be moving into the watery sign of Scorpio. This is the area of your chart devoted to home and family, which is very apt. This planet will be stirring up a good deal of activity, so it's quite clear that you are the one who is providing the fare. But do make sure that others pitch in too. After all, this time of the year is about giving but that doesn't mean only for those born under the sign of Leo.

25 MONDAY Today is the day of the New Moon and because of this your Christmas arrangements should run as smooth as silk. People are willing to be more helpful than usual and it looks as if you are about to give them one or two rather delightful presents too. If you're spending Christmas away from home, you're going to be spoiled rotten.

26 TUESDAY The Moon is in Capricorn, and so it's quite likely that many of you may be suffering from that awful Christmas bloated feeling. If this should apply to you, then try to plan a quiet time. Explain how you feel to your loved ones and then you can become the life and soul of the party later on in the day.

27 WEDNESDAY Jupiter is lining up with Mars, and so there's a lively feel about this particular day. Many of you may be taking part in sports, or perhaps just being a spectator. Wherever you go, and whoever you are spending time with, it's bound to be a day of joy and happiness.

28 THURSDAY Loved ones have high expectations of you but you cannot meet all their demands. Let the stars be your signal to call a halt to a difficult situation. You may think any provocation will cause disruption at home, but the reverse is true. A few sharp words will now prevent a major scene later on.

29 FRIDAY On paper others may be better equipped to handle certain financial matters. But you seem to have an instinct and the aspects today highlight a power struggle you have every chance of winning. Keep one ace up your sleeve.

30 SATURDAY You seem to be caught up in a tug-of-war concerning partnership matters. You know the facts and are following them to the letter. That's where your greatest strength lies. Those who want to bend the rules do so at their own risk. All eyes are upon you, so be seen at your brightest.

31 SUNDAY Everyone else seems to have gained the upper hand. However, you are about to learn how to use untapped resources to regain control. Conflicts concerning money or romance cannot be resolved until you are in a better frame of mind. The planets are urging you to come out of your corner fighting. Be sure you channel out some of that energy in having fun this evening.

Happy New Year!

Advertisement

Your Birth Chart by Teri King

A Book of Life

Simply fill in your details on the form below for an interpretation of your birth chart compiled by TERI KING. Your birth chart will be supplied bound and personalized. Each chart costs £30.00 sterling – add £1.50 sterling for postage if you live outside the UK. Please make your cheque or postal order (cash is not accepted) payable to *Kingstar* and send, together with your form, to the following address: 6 Elm Grove Road, Barnes, London SW13 0BT, England.

Date of birth .... Time of birth ....

Place of birth .... Country of birth ....

Name ....

Address ....

....

.... Postcode ....

A birth chart also makes an ideal present! Why not include, on a separate sheet, the details of a friend or member of your family? Include £30.00 for each extra chart.